Securing Biometrics Applications

Securing Biometrics Applications

by

Charles A. Shoniregun
University of East London
UK

and

Stephen Crosier
University of East London
UK

 Springer

Charles A. Shoniregun
Reader in Computing
KNURE/KSAC Distinguished Professor
School of Computing and Technology
University of East London
University Way
LONDON, UK
c.shoniregun@uel.ac.uk

Stephen Crosier
School of Computing and Technology
University of East London
University Way
LONDON, UK
Steve.crosier@ntlworld.com

Securing Biometrics Applications by Charles A. Shoniregun and Stephen Crosier

ISBN 978-1-4419-4350-7   e-ISBN-13: 978-0-387-69933-2

Printed on acid-free paper.

9 8 7 6 5 4 3 2 1

springer.com

DEDICATIONS

To our families and friends

TABLE OF CONTENTS

LIST OF FIGURES

LIST OF TABLES

LIST OF CONTRIBUTORS AND ORGANISATIONS

Alex Logvynovskiy	e-Centre for Infonomics, UK
Harvey Freeman	Booze Allen Hamilton, USA
Caterina Scoglio	Kansas State University, Kansas, USA
Maaruf Ali	Oxford Brooks University, UK
Victoria Repka	Kharkov National University of Radioelectronics, Ukraine
Vyacheslav Grebenyuk	Kharkov National University of Radioelectronics, Ukraine
Kia Makki	Florida International University, Miami, USA
Niki Passinou	Florida International University, Miami, USA
Ann-Sofi Höijenstam	Precise Biometrics AB
Terry Cook	City University, USA.
Jen-Yao Chung	IBM Watson Research Centre, USA
Liang-Jie (LJ) Zhang	IBM Watson Research Centre, USA
Patrick Hung	University of Ontario, Institute of Technology, Canada
Dragana Martinovic	University of Windsor, Canada
Victor Ralevich	Sheridan Institute of Technology and Advance Learning, Canada
Pit Pichappan	Annamalai University, India

InternetSecuirty.com
National Security Agency, USA
National Centre for State court, USA
Centre for Unified Biometrics and Sensors. University of Buffalo, USA
International Biometric Society, USA
CERT Coordination Centre, USA
Cisco, USA
Dell, UK
e-Centre for Infonomics, UK
InternetSecurity.org.uk, UK
Microsoft Corp, USA
Sun Microsystems, Inc., USA
University of Massachusetts, USA

PREFACE

This study investigates the security of biometric applications, the opportunities and the challenges to our society. The increasing threats to national security by terrorists have led to the explosive popularity of biometric technologies. The biometric devices are now available to capture biometric measurements of the fingerprints, palm, retinal, keystroke, voice and facial expressions. The accuracy of these measurements varies, which has a direct impacts on the levels of security they offer. With the need to combat the problems related to identify theft and other security issues, society will have to compromise between security and personal freedoms. Without doubt the 21st century has brought about a techno-society that requires more secure and accurate measures.

We have also identified the key impacts of biometric security applications and ways of minimising the risk liability of individual biometrics profile that would be kept in database. The individual identification and verification have long been accomplished by showing something you have (driving licence or a passport) and required something you know (password or a PIN). The possibility of the back-end authentication process (in a networked situation) being compromised by the passing of illegal data may represent a point of vulnerability. The authentication engine and its associated interface could be fooled. It is necessary to suggest a measure of risk to the biometric system in use, especially when the authentication engine may not be able to verify that it is receiving a bona fide live transaction data (and not a data stream from another source).

More recently, the biometric identification technologies have been adopted into upmarket devices (Laptop mobile phones, cars, building access control, national identity cards, and fast-track clearance through immigration. Thus biometrics is becoming increasingly common in establishments that require high security (government departments, public meeting places, and multinational organisations) but a highly accurate biometric system can reject authorised users, fail to identify known users, identify users incorrectly, or allow unauthorised person to verify as known users. In addition, if a third-party network is utilised as part of the overall biometric system, for example using the Internet to connect remotely to corporate networks, the end-to-end connection between host controller and back-end application server should be carefully considered. In most cases, biometric system cannot determine if an individual has established a fraudulent identity, or is posing as another individual during biometrics enrolment process. An individual with a fake passport may be able to use the passport as the basis of enrolment in a biometric system. The system can only verify that the individual is who he or she claimed to be during enrolment. To solve these problems, we proposed the Shoniregun and Crosier Securing Biometrics Applications Model (SCSBAM).

Furthermore, the success of using biometrics technologies as a means of personal identification is more assuring and comfortable because access, authentication and authorisation is granted based on a unique feature of an individuals physiological, biological or behavioural characteristic. It is tempting to think of biometrics as being sci-fi futuristic technology that we should in the near future use together with solar-powered cars, and other fiendish devices—but who knows?

ACKNOWLEDGEMENTS

It is difficult to acknowledge all the people that have directly or indirectly contributed to this book. But some names cannot be forgotten —many thanks to our editor Susan Lagerstrom-Fife, publishing director Jennifer Evans and Rudiger Gebauer for their support. Indeed, those kind reminders and useful comments from Susan and Sharon are all appreciated.

A special thank you to Dr Alex Logvynovskiy of e-Centre for Infonomics, for his never-ending contribution.

Undoubtedly, our reflection to past experiences both in the commercial sector and academia has help to bridge the gap in our understanding of the impacts of biometric security applications and ways of minimising the risk liability of individual biometrics profile. We would also like to acknowledge our appreciation to the following organisations: Precise Biometrics AB, IR Recognition systems Inc, Bio-key International, Identix, SAF Solution Enterprise, Wonder Net and Executive Agent for Biometrics.

Our sincere thanks to all the organisations that voluntarily participated in our search for knowledge.

Chapter 1

RESEARCH OVERVIEW AND BIOMETRIC TECHNOLOGIES

1.   INTRODUCTION

The purpose of this study is to identify the key impacts of biometric security applications and ways of minimising the risk liability of individual biometrics profile that would be kept in the database system/server. The term biometrics was derived from the Greek words bio (life) and metric (to measure). The concept of biometrics is dated back to over a thousand years where potters in East Asia placed their fingers on their wares as an early form of branding. In the 14th century explorer Joao de Barros reported that the Chinese merchants were stamping children's palm prints and footprints on paper with ink to distinguish the young children from one another. This is one of the earliest known cases of biometrics in use and is still being used today.

'Degrees of freedom represent the number of independent varieties of a deviation. If 100 shred strips of paper were randomly dropped from the same distance, for example the end result would differ each time, and the likelihood of getting the same result is almost impossible.'

—Chirillo J, and Blaul S, 2003

In different parts of the world up until the late 1800s, identification was largely relied upon by photographic memory and biometrics has moved from a single method (fingerprinting) to more than ten discreet methods. As the industry grows however, so does the public concern over privacy issues. Laws and regulations continue to be drafted and standards are beginning to be developed. Biometrics is rapidly evolving technology which has been widely used in forensics, but presently it is adopted in broad applications used in Banks, electronic commerce, access control welfare, disbursement programme to deter multiple claims, health care, immigration applications, national ID Card to provide a unique ID to citizens and passport, airport terminals to allow passengers easy and quicker check-in and also to enhance security. Other technologies are seen as cutting-edge, but their accuracy remains questionable.

2.   RESEARCH RATIONALE

The Department of Defence (DOD) set out Password Management Guideline in 1985. The Guideline codified the state of the use of passwords at that time, the Guideline provided recommendations for how individuals should select and handle passwords. As a result of DOD Password Management Guideline, computer users are told to periodically change their passwords. Many systems expire a user's password after an established period of weeks or months when they prompt user to change the password, however some users tend to forget and they are logged out, and the only way for them to get back in the system was a call to the IT helpdesk, which can be flooded with calls. The help desk staff may end up spending a disproportionately large amount of time fixing problems with passwords. Some systems tend to use password hashing for obscuring a password cryptographically; conversely, hashing makes it impractical to retrieve a user's password once forgotten.

Insecure authentication methods often leads to loss of confidential information, denial of services, lack of trust and issues with integrity of data and information contents. The value of a reliable user authentication is not limited to just computer access only, but to many other interconnected systems. The existing techniques of user authentications (user ID cards, passwords, chip and pin) are subject to several limitations. For example the main security weakness of password and token-based authentication mechanisms is that the awareness or possession of an item does not distinguish a person uniquely. The authentication policy based on the combination of user id and password has become inadequate. The biometric can provide much more accurate and reliable user authentication method by identifying an individual based on their physiological or behavioural characteristics (inherent features, which are difficult to duplicate and almost impossible to share) (see Tables 1–1 and 1–2 for further details). Using biometrics makes it possible to establish an identity based on 'who you are', rather than the validity of biometric accuracy by 'what you possess' (photo ID or credit cards and passport) or 'what you remember' (password) (Campbell et al, 2003).

Table 1–1. Validity of biometric accuracy

Biometric system	Accuracy	Ease of use
Fingerprint	High	Medium
Hand Geometry	Medium	High
Voice	Medium	High
Retinal	High	Low
Iris	Medium	Medium
Signature	Medium	Medium
Face	Low	High

The biometric systems establish an aspect of user convenience that may not be possible using traditional security techniques. For example, users maintaining different passwords for different applications may find it challenging to remember the password of each specific application. In some instances, the user might even forget the password, thereby requiring the help desk to intervene and perhaps reset the password for that user while the biometric link an event to a person, which prevents any form of impersonation.

3. RESEARCH HYPOTHESIS

To identify and minimise the security of biometric applications a number of leading research questions were emerged to test the hypotheses:

i. What precisely constitutes biometrics?

ii. Is classification and taxonomy of biometrics possible?

iii. What are the impacts of biometrics on society?

iv. What constitutes the failure of biometrics technology?

v. Is security an issue for biometrics users?

However, knowledge can be very hypocritical at the beginning but always satisfactory when results are achieved. The following hypotheses have been formulated based on the above questions and the literature review (which includes ongoing access to online resources and laboratory experiments). All we can say is that we do not have evidence to reject or accept the emerging hypothesis.

Hypothesis 1:

- Null hypothesis (H_0^1): Classification and taxonomy of biometrics are unattainable.

- Alternative (H_A^1): Classification and taxonomy of biometrics are attainable.

Hypothesis 2:

- Null hypothesis (H_0^2): Biometrics is not complementary to generic security approach.

- Alternative (H_A^2): Biometrics is complementary to generic security approach.

Hypothesis 3:

- Null hypothesis (H_0^3): Absolute security is unattainable on biometrics

- Alternative (H_A^3): Absolute security is attainable on biometrics.

On a serious note, making biometrics applications secured has been a hot debate for many years. The key issues in securing biometrics applications are contained in the generic architecture of the technologies that are adopted. The generic security implementations such as password and keys have been in place for a long time but unlike today, the intermediate systems at the time had no requirement to access multi-platform and millions of interconnected technologies. As the technology advances much more sophisticated system have been introduced, the deployment of biometrics has raises some issues, which must be addressed. These issues are the rediscovery of where and when do we require biometrics technology. There has been an increase in the number of devices that interoperates with biometrics to ensure that compliant implementations include the services and management interfaces needed to meet the security requirements of a broad user population.

Generally speaking, wherever there is a password or PIN used in an application or system, it could be possibly replaced by biometrics. But it varies according to the application requirements. However, applications can be characterised by the following characteristics Nalini, et al., 1999:

- Attended vs. unattended.

- Overt vs. covert.

- Cooperative vs. non-cooperative.

- Scalable (means that the database being scalable with no appreciable performance degradation) vs. non-scalable

- Acceptable vs. non-acceptable.

The biometrics technologies can be used to verify (*identification:* who am I?) or to identify (*verification* or *authentication:* am I whom I claim to be?) an individual. The biometrics identification determines who a person is. It involves measuring individual's characteristics and mapping it with users profile stored in the database. The main purpose of positive identification is to prevent multiple users from claiming a single identity. In positive identification method, the user normally claims an identity by giving a name or an ID number, and then submits a biometric measure. Once submitted, it's matched with the previously submitted measure to verify that the current enrolled user is under the claimed identity (Wayman, 2000). These tasks can be achieved through many non-biometric alternatives in such applications as ID cards, PINs and passwords. Depending on the situation or the environment where it's installed, positive identification biometric method can be made voluntary and those not wishing to use biometrics can verify identity in other ways. The biometrics identification method can require a large amount of processing power especially if the database is very large. It is often used in determining the identity of a suspect from crime scene information. There are two types of identification: positive and negative. Positive identification expects a match between the biometric presented and the template, it is designed to make sure that the person is in the database. While the negative identification is set up to ensure that the person is not in the database, more so, it can take the form of watch list where a match triggers a notice to the appropriate authority for action.

On the other hand, biometrics *verification* or *authentication* is determines that an individual is who they say they are. It involves taking the measured characteristic and compares them with previously recorded data of the person. The main function of negative identification in an organisation is to prevent claims of multiple identities by a single user. In negative identification, the user who enrols for biometric authentication claims that he or she have not been previously enrolled and submits a biometric measure, which is compared to all others in the system database. If the user's claim of non-enrolment is verified, that means a match is not found (Wayman, 2000). At the moment there are no reliable non-biometric alternatives in such applications, hence the use of biometrics in negative identification applications must be mandatory in places where it's important. The biometrics *verification* or *authentication* method requires less processing power and time. It is often used for accessing places or information, depending on the application domain; a biometric can either be an online or an offline system. To verify an individual's identity a 1:1 check is made between the biometric data and the biometric template obtained during enrolment (see Figure 1–1 for diagrammatic illustration). For any biometric system to be effective the data should be stored securely and not be vulnerable to theft, abuse or tampering. The data should also be free of errors to prevent false positive and negative results, and the user must be confident that the system is reliable and secure.

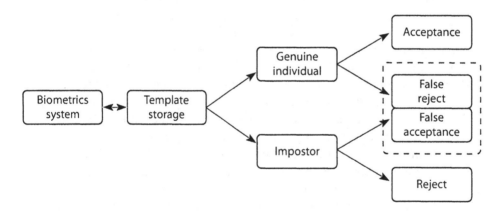

Figure 1–1. Generic biometric system process

The vast amount of data that is now held on everyone and the increases forecast for the future means that it is conceivably possible for people whereabouts to be traced through their use of information. With the need to combat the increasing problems related to identity theft and other security issues, the society will have to make a choice between security and personal freedoms. Biometrics can be incorporated at the point of sale, thereby enabling consumers to enrol their payment options (cheques, loyalty cards, credit and debit cards) into a secure electronic account that is protected by, and accessed with, a unique physical attribute. All biometric systems require an authorised user to register with the system. This involves the person supplying the relevant biometric information needed by the system, which is then converted to data that can be stored on a database. For biometrics to be globally adopted there is a need for international standards compatibility.

4. CONCEPTUAL RESEARCH CONTEXT

From the late 1990's, governments and private organisations have developed a particular interest in biometrics and are actively funding projects involving biometrics technology. Hence, biometrics became an independent research field. It has been observed that the identity established by biometric is not an absolute 'yes' or 'no', instead it is gives a level of confidence. The Law enforcers department, matching finger images against criminal records has always been an important way to identify criminals or trace a person to a crime that that has been committed. But the manual process of matching is difficult and takes time. The Federal Bureau of Investigation (FBI) in late 1960s began to automatically check fingerprint images, and by the mid-1970s a number of automatic finger scanning systems were in operation (Zhang, et al., 2006). The Identimat pioneered the application of hand geometry and set a path for biometrics technologies as a whole. The developments in hardware, with faster processing power and high memory capability have led to advancements in the biometrics technology evolution.

With rapid growth in electronic transactions, there has been an absolute demand for biometrics technologies that enabled secure transactions but if biometrics are to become widely implemented by government and the private sectors, the public must trust that their privacy cannot be compromised and the information will not be misused. When biometric data is provided to an organisation the public should be made aware of who can access their data and how it can be used. One question would be, if fingerprints were provided for identity cards and passports— *would another government agency (such as the police) have unrestricted access to the database?* In the United State the fingerprints taken at immigration are automatically added to the FBI database. Therefore, organisations most trusted to control private data were government agencies and banks, so if biometric systems are introduced a number of questions needs to be answered:

• Who will administer biometrics profile?

• How should it be administered?

- What features should be required?

- What should be done to create awareness of trust?

In 2006 a survey was conducted by UNISYS on public perceptions of identity management. The study looked at Europe, North America, Latin America and the Asia-Pacific regions, there was a willingness amongst the respondents to share personal data in order to prove or verify their identity. The rates of acceptance vary between the regions. The findings are summarised as follows:

- In North America and Asia-Pacific respondents were more likely to share more personal data with both a trusted private business and with government, than were the respondents in Europe and Latin America.

- Respondents in Europe, North America and the Asia-Pacific regions were more willing to share personal information with governments, while in Latin America the reverse was true.

- In all regions individuals were more willing to share substantially more personal data in order to receive enhanced verification capabilities, e.g., for a multi-purpose identity credential which could be used for a number of functions.

- The data which people would be most willing to share are name, address and telephone number, but they were not willing to give information about race, religion or credit card number.

- The most important functions of a multi-functional identity credential were to access buildings, Internet accounts and immigration.

- Most individuals would prefer the data to be held on a chip on an identity card. There was also acceptance for incorporating data as a biometric within a cellular phone. When asked about the chip being implanted within the body, the acceptance rate was very low.

- It is also important that the multi purpose identity criteria should be interoperable across borders.

The UNISYS survey revealed that, the most accepted biometrics profile were fingerprints and voice, with iris being the least accepted. There is no doubt that the future assessment of biometrics will be based on security, convenient, efficient and speed.

4.1   What is biometrics

The Bertillonage system was developed in the 1890's by a Paris police desk clerk, an anthropologist named Alphonse Bertillon, as a method of identifying convicted criminals. This method of identification became the primary method for identifying criminals in the late 1800's. Criminals are very dubious, so often gave different aliases each time they were arrested, this became a problem on how best to identifying repeated offenders Bertillion realised that even if names changed, certain elements of the body remained fixed (such as the size of the skull or the length of their fingers). Based on the assertion adult bones do not change after the age of 20. The system was a success, identifying hundreds of repeated offenders. It was adopted world wide by the police authorities until 1903, when two identical (within the tolerances) measurements were obtained for two different persons at the Fort Leavenworth prison, then Bertillonage accuracy became questionable.

The biometric systems recognise a person by physiological or behavioural characteristics. This data is then studied by mathematical and statistical methods. In information technology these methods are being used to develop identification methods for biological traits such as fingerprints and retinal scans, to aid in authentication of the user to increase the levels of security that can be achieved. The following diagram (see Figure 1–2 for diagrammatic illustration) shows a generic model of a biometric system, showing the stages, which have to be gone through to get a final decision.

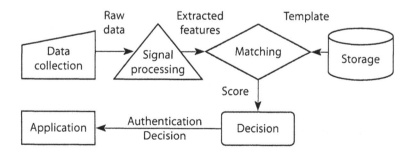

Figure 1–2. Generic biometric system model

The biometric systems are used to 'verify' or to 'identify' an individual. To verify an individual's identity a 1:1 check is made between the biometric data and the biometric template obtained during enrolment. To identify means to do a 1 to many search between the offered biometric data and a collection of templates from all of those enrolled on the system. The following are generic definitions of biometrics:

- Biometrics is the development of statistical and mathematical methods applicable to data analysis problems in the biological sciences.

- Biometrics is characteristic of the body as a method to code or scramble/de-scramble data.

- Biometrics is used to identify people based on their biological traits.

- Biometrics is the measurement and matching of biological characteristics such as fingerprint images, hand geometry, facial recognition, etc.

- Biometrics is the application of statistics and mathematics to problems with a biological component."

- Biometrics uses a unique physical attribute of your body, such as your fingerprint or iris, to identify and verify you.

- Biometrics is unique personal characteristics"

- Biometrics, or bio-identification, is the practice of measuring physical characteristics of a person to verify their identity.

- Biometrics = identification/verification of persons based on the unique physiological or behavioural features of humans.

- Biometrics is defined as the automated recognition of individuals based on their biological or behavioural characteristics.

- Biometrics any human physical or biological feature that can be measured and used for the purpose of automated or semi-automated identification.

- Biometrics is strongly linked to a stored identity to the physical person.

- Biometrics is measurable, physiological and/or behavioural characteristics that verify the identity of an individual.

- Biometrics is the automated use of physiological or behavioural characteristics to determine or verify identity.

In terms of simplicity, biometric are passive in that it only requires an interaction between the person and the system this eliminate time wasting when interacting with other person. With the increasing use of computers networks, electronic transfer of confidential information and high sensitive government places, it is necessary to restrict access. The Table 1–2 is adopted from Jain *et al.*, (1999) to show what particular body characteristics are suitable for biometric.

Table 1–2. Seven pillars of biometric wisdom

Universality	All human beings are endowed with the same physical characteristics - such as fingers, iris, face, DNA – which can be used for identification
Distinctiveness	For each person these characteristics are unique, and thus constitute a distinguishing feature
Permanence	These characteristics remain largely unchanged throughout a person's life
Collectability	A person's unique physical characteristics need to be collected in a reasonably easy fashion for quick identification
Performance	The degree of accuracy of identification must be quite high before the system can be operational
Acceptability	Applications will not be successful if the public offers strong and continuous resistance to biometrics
Resistance to Circumvention	In order to provide added security, a system needs to be harder to circumvent than existing identity management systems

A system protecting confidential information, or items of value, puts strong security demands on the identification. Biometry provides a user-friendly method for this identification and is becoming a competitor for current identification mechanisms, especially for electronic transactions. Some manufacturers claim to use even more exotic detection methods and techniques but is advisable not to use security by obscurity (trust that, by keeping specifications secret, the system will not be broken) because obscurity can make it more difficult for people to break the system in a brief period after introduction, most systems can be reverse engineered or worked.

4.2   Types of biometrics

There are more than ten different techniques available to identify and verify a person based on biometrics. These techniques are categorised under two

major types of biometrics: the physical biometrics can be used for either identification or verification while the behavioural biometrics is generally used
for verification. These two types of biometrics are briefly outlined below (see
chapter 2 for further discussion).

i. Physical biometrics consists of the following:

  • Bertillonage: measuring body lengths (no longer used).

  • Fingerprint: analyse the fingertip patterns.

  • Facial recognition: measuring facial characteristics.

  • Hand geometry: measuring the shape of the hand.

  • Iris scan: analyse the features of colour ring of the eye.

  • Retinal scan: analyse the blood vessels in the eye.

  • Vascular patterns: analyse the vein patterns.

  • Ear shape: cartilaginous tissue.

  • DNA: analyse the genetic makeup.

  • Data watermarking: is a method rather than a physical attribute: store/
    hide biometric information.

It worth noting that since the 1990s, iris, retinal, face, voice, signature, palm-
print and DNA technologies have joined the biometric family.

ii. Behavioural biometrics consists of the following:

  • Voice recognition: analyse the vocal behaviour.

  • Signature: analyse the signature dynamics.

  • Keystroke: measures the time of the typing space.

  • Gait: analyse the way in which a person walks.

The studies published to date on biometric security are based on evaluations of false rejection and false acceptance rates. Moreover, using biometric access protection procedures in a Windows 98 or Windows ME environment is not secured; users' should immediately block all avenues whereby regular enrolment might be bypassed. Biometrics has been applied in many areas, from finance to identity cards to access control. The Tables 1–3 to 1–10 shows the evolution of most common biometrics.

Table 1–3. Fingerprint

Late 1800's	The points and characteristics to identify fingerprints were defined by Sir Francis Galton.
1960's	The transition of fingerprint identification to automation began.
1969	The FBI began to push for the automation of the fingerprint identification process.
1975	The FBI funded the development of fingerprint scanners for automated classifiers and minutiae extraction technology.
1970's to 1980's	NIST led the development of automated methods of digitising inked fingerprints and the effects of image compression on image quality, classification, extraction of minutiae and matching.
1980's	M40 algorithm was developed as the FBI's first operational matching algorithm.
1981	Five Automated Fingerprint Identification Systems {AFIS} were deployed.
1994	Integrated Automated Fingerprint Identification Systems {IAFIS} was developed.
1999	Lockheed Martin was selected to build the AFIS segment of the FBI's IAFIS project. The major IAFIS components were operational by 1999.
2003	The Fingerprint Vendor Technology Evaluation (FpTVE) was initiated to evaluate the accuracy of the available fingerprint recognition systems.
2004	The US-VISIT program became operational as a security measure at entry points to the USA. A photograph of everyone entering the country is taken at passport control and is checked against a database. The system verifies whether the visitor has been to the USA before whether they are a security risk {Including having outstanding warrants} or has previously overstayed their visa.

Table 1–4. Face recognition

1960's	A semi automated system was developed which required an administrator to locate features such as eyes, ears, nose and mouth on a photograph. The system then calculated distances and ratios to a common reference point.
1970's	The system was automated by Goldstein, Harman and Leck, who used 21 specific subjective markers such as hair colour and lip thickness.
1988	Kirby and Sirovich applied principle component analysis.
1991	Turk and Pentland discovered the use of eigenface techniques.

1993-1997	Face Recognition Technology {FERET} Evaluation was sponsored by the Defence Advanced Research Products Agency.
2000, 2002 and 2006	Face Recognition Vendor Tests {FRVT} took place.
2001	A trial at the NFL Super Bowl captured surveillance images and compared them to a database of digital facial images.
2004	The US-VISIT program became operational as a security measure at entry points to the USA. A photograph of everyone entering the country is taken at passport control and is checked against a database. The system verifies whether the visitor has been to the USA before whether they are a security risk {Including having outstanding warrants} or has previously overstayed their visa.
2006	Face recognition grand challenge.

Table 1–5. Hand geometry

1980's	Hand geometry was first developed.
1985	The first patented hand geometry system was developed by David Sidlauskas.
1986	First commercial hand geometry recognition system became available.
1991	An evaluation of biometric identification devices was carried out. The relative performances of multiple biometric devices, including hand geometry were assessed.
1996	Hand geometry systems were used to control and protect physical access to the Olympic village in Atlanta.
1996	The INSPASS Hand Geometry Data was evaluated to determine the effect, which a threshold has on the operation of the system. The false accept and false reject rates were established as a a function of the threshold. They were presented as an estimate of the Receiver Operating Characteristics {ROC} curve for the INSPASS system.
1990's to present	Hand Geometry systems have been implemented by many companies to complement time clocks for time and attendance purposes.
2004	Finger geometry was introduced to Walt Disney World in Florida to facilitate entrance to the park and to identify the holders of season tickets to prevent fraud.

Table 1–6. Palm print

1858	Sir William Herschel who worked for the Indian civil service, recorded a handprint on the back of a contract for each worker, to distinguish employees from others who might claim to be employees when pay day arrives.
1994	A Hungarian company built the first AFIS system to support palm prints.
1997	A US company bought the Hungarian palm system.
2000's	The largest database of palm prints is held in Australia. The Australian National Automated Fingerprint identification System {NAFIS} includes 4.8 million palm prints.

2004   Connecticut, Rhode Island and California established statewide palm print databases, which allowed law enforcement agencies in each state to submit unidentified latent palm prints to be searched against each other's databases of known offenders.

Table 1–7. Iris recognition

1936	An ophthalmologist, Frank Burch fist proposed using iris patterns as a method to recognise an individual.
1985	Flom and Safir were ophthalmologists who proposed the concept that no two irises were the same.
1985	Dr's Flom and Safir were awarded a patent for their iris recognition concept.
1993	Work to test and deliver a prototype unit was begun by the Defence Nuclear Agency.
1994	Dr Daugman was awarded a patent for his automated iris recognition algorithm.
1995	Dr's Flom, Safir and Daugman joined forces to produce a prototype
1995	The first commercial products were released.
2005	The patent covering the basic concept of iris recognition expired, which provided other companies with marketing opportunities for their own iris recognition algorithms.
2011	The patent on 'IrisCodes' iris recognition developed by Dr Daugman will expire.

Table 1–8. Vascular pattern

1992	Dr K. Shimizu published a paper on optical trans-body imaging and potential optical CT scanning applications.
1996	K.Yakamoto and K. Shimuzu continued research.
2000	The first research paper abut the use of vascular patterns for biometric recognition was published.
2000	The first commercial devices became available; they used subcutaneous blood vessel patterns in the back of the hand as the vascular pattern.

Table 1–9. Speech verification

1960	Professor Gunnar Fant published a model describing the physiological components of acoustic speech production, based on the analysis of x-rays of individuals making specific phonic sounds.
1970	Dr Joseph Perkell used motion x-rays and included the tongue and jaw to expand the Fant model.
1976	Texas Instruments built a prototype system, which was tested by the US Air Force and the MITRE Corporation.

Mid 1980's National Institute of Standards and Technology {NIST} developed the NIST speech group to study and promote the use of speech processing techniques.
1996   National Security Agency funded and the NIST started hosting the annual evaluation. The NIST Speaker Recognition Evaluation Workshop aimed to foster the continued advancement of the speaker recognition community.

Table 1–10. Dynamic signature recognition

1965   First signature recognition system was developed.
1970's Research continued into the development of static or geometric characteristics (the appearance of the signature) rather than the dynamic characteristics (features such as pressure and speed at which the signature is written).
1970's With the availability of better acquisition systems, with the use of touch sensitive technologies interest began to increase in the dynamic characteristics of the signature.
1977   The first patent was awarded for a 'personal identification apparatus', which was capable of acquiring dynamic pressure information.

Moreover, some biometric identification systems are still in a development phase and there is no real mass market, so no significant economies of scale are available yet. This should change once a sufficient number of large-scale applications are up and running. The type of biometrics to be adopted is determined by the level of security, which is required, *how many people are going to be using it and the ease of use?* A balance must be struck between the costs of installation and operation and the savings to be made if it is installed. The methods of identification to be applied have to be carefully selected. Global standards must be introduced for software and hardware to be easily interconnected (see section 7 for further discussion).

5.   CURRENT TECHNOLOGY FOR BIOMETRICS

Computer manufacturers are now building systems that incorporate fingerprint and eye scanner software into their machines. Biometrics could be a major security system for the future in the battle against online crime. It is basically concerned with digitally encoding physical attributes of the users voice, eye, face or hand to a unique ID. Such an ID is now used for clearance into buildings. The biometrics identification could be used in the future to secure online transaction(s). The foolproof of authenticating someone is by physical identification, therefore, making it impossible for fraud to occur (unless of course, the hackers turned to kidnapping!). Despite the fact that it would be an expensive process to scan every customer with a biometric scanner, many companies, especially the financial ones, will probably adopt this strategy anyway. Overall, the cost of biometrically scanning customers may be less expensive than the costs incurred by fraud in the long term. The Infineon Technologies AG and Veridicom Inc. have produced finger-scanning chips that can be embedded into a computer keyboard or mouse to verify authentication of the user by fingerprint ID. As technology becomes cheaper, it is not impractical to think that people may have chips implanted into computer keyboards 'as standard'. Keyware Technologies Inc and Proton World International have in turn produced a smart card that can identify the authenticity of the user. When validity is confirmed, the smart card then allows release of credit card and user details to the website. This technology is really not as 'sci-fi' as one can imagine. Already ING Direct, Canada, has issued fingerprint biometric security systems to their online banking customers. ING Direct has distributed computer mice to a selected group of customers with embedded fingerprint chips. Results from trials will determine whether biometrics is a viable security option. However, initially this type of technology will be very difficult to install due to the systems required for it and the expense of it. In the longer term, the costs should decrease and one day it may be possible for everyone owning a computer to have the technology for trouble free purchasing on the web. The UK's Barclays Bank has been using finger scan technology for employee access to buildings since 1996 and is also currently involved in a pilot program for PC log-ins to the corporate networks. In 1998, Nationwide Building Society became the first organisation in the world to trial iris recognition technology supplied by ATM manufacturer NCR. 91% of their customers said they would chose iris identification over PIN's or signatures in the future (Desmarais, 2000; White, 2001).

6. ENROLMENT

A considerably wide variety of technologies can be described as biometric access systems, and they all work along the same principles. Their purpose is to deny access to a target (usually a room or a computer network) for individuals who have not been specifically authorised access. In order to enrol a biometric system would require access to the record of the biometric characteristic that is created during an initial enrolment routine when the user's biometric characteristic is sampled and the enrolment template is created and stored in the database system (see Figure 1–3 for diagrammatic illustration).

The most critical information during enrolment is the true identity and set of privileges of the user. Subsequent identification and verifications will automatically reference the enrolment information (enrolment template). The enrolment templates enabled the future comparisons of individual biometric profile possible. The identification system searches for enrolment templates, which should be stored in a centralised database system. A verification system access the enrolment template stored in centralised database or stored in a transportable medium assigned to the user. After the user has been enrolled, he/she has access privileges to a protected resource. At each access point, the enrolled user submits identification for verification using specified biometric device. The identification sample is processed to produce an authentication template. The verification system is use for locating the enrolment template associated with the identity stored in the database. The access privileges are awarded if the templates match and also the privileges vary from one system to the other. The types of access systems are as follow:

- Physical access system is an electric signal, to unlock a door.

- Logical access system is usually the release of a stored encrypted password to gain access to an application. The logical access privilege stored encrypted password to be released and used in place of a user-entered password.

The computation algorithm for an access system looks for similarities between the templates to decide whether the templates are a matching set or not. It is possible to control the number of templates that have similarities but if the templates fail to match, access privileges are not awarded. A record of the failed access attempt is kept in a log that can be reviewed. The templates sometimes fail; this does not necessarily indicate a malicious intrusion attempt, but it simply means that the individual biometric profile that was taken to create the authentication template was not a good quality. The authentication template cannot technically be used directly as a fit for purpose since each new authentication template will have some variation from the enrolment template on file. Therefore, the systems have to compare the authentication template and the enrolment template to determine the match. The condition of finding a match is equivalent to having a key. From the user's perspective using a biometric system replaces passwords, but in reality using a biometric does not usually replace password but enhance the system security.

A simple biometric system has four important components:

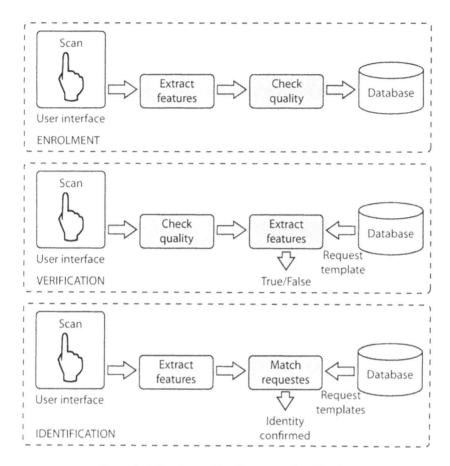

Figure 1–3. Enrolment: identification and verification

i. The sensor, which captures the biometric data of an individual. An example is a fingerprint sensor that captures fingerprint impressions of a user.

ii. Feature Extraction is the stage in which the acquired data is processed to extract feature values. For example, the position and orientation of minutiae points in a fingerprint image would be computed in the feature extraction module of a fingerprint system.

iii. Matching phase is carried out when the feature values are compared against those in the template by generating a matching score. For example, in this module, the number of matching minutiae between the query and the template can be computed and treated as a matching score.

iv. Decision-making phase is done when the user's claimed identity is either accepted or rejected based on the matching score generated in the matching module.

The biometrics enrolment can be divided into *enrolment and identification*. The enrolment phase is responsible for enrolling an individual into the biometric system. During the enrolment phase, biometric characteristics of an individual are first scanned to produce a raw digital representation of the characteristics. In order to facilitate matching, a feature extract to generate a compact but expressive representation, called a template, further processes the raw digital representation of. The template may then be stored in a central database or recorded on a magnetic card or smart card (and issued to an individual) depending on the nature of the application. The identification phase is responsible for identifying individuals at the point of access. During the operation phase, the biometric reader captures the characteristics of individuals to be identified and converts it to a digital format, which is further processed by the extractor to produce the same representation, the ensuing image is fed to the feature matcher which compares it against the templates to establish the identity (Hong, 1998; Woodward et al, 2003).

7.   STANDARDS

The NIST and the Biometric Consortium have established this Working Group to support advancement of technically efficient and compatible biometric technology solutions on a national and international basis and to promote and encourage exchange of information and collaborative efforts between users and private industry in all things biometric. The Working Group consists of ninety organisations representing biometric vendors, system developers, and information assurance organisations, commercial end users, universities, Government agencies, National Labs and industry organisations. For biometrics work effectively it must be compatible. To resolve the compatibility issues, the European BioSec Consortium in cooperation with other standards bodies around the world is working on developing a number of standards. The aim is to develop a comprehensive set of standards for the application of biometrics, which should help in the adoption of biometric technologies for improved security. Howarth (2000) detailed the key standardisation issues involved in the development of biometric:

i. *Harmonised biometric vocabulary and definitions*: It seems obvious that everyone involved in the field of biometrics should be reading from the same page, but the meaning of the words on that page may vary widely owing to differences in culture and language. The BioSec participants are working on a harmonised vocabulary in the hope that this will form part of the ISO standard SC37 for biometrics.

ii. *Technical interfaces*: Since multiple vendors will be involved in the provision of biometric technology systems, a reference model needs to be developed to standardise the necessary application interfaces and interactions. Standards being developed include those for security; conformance testing and data exchange to ensure that biometric information can be transferred among networks, and hence used in remote access scenarios for such things as securing transactions.

iii. *Data interchange formats*: Standards need to be developed for how all the different types of biometric identifiers in use are encoded and represented. This involves defining a common data structure, including notation and transfer formats, so that data can be presented in a common format worldwide.

iv. *Functional architecture and related profiles*: Here, work is being done to develop a functional architecture that incorporates standards being developed in biometrics. The aim is to ensure that the various standards are bound together in a way that actually aids the functional operation of biometric systems in real-life scenarios, making certain that the right options in the standards are selected for a specific application.

v. *Testing*: The emphasis in this area is on the development of standard methodologies and metrics for testing biometric systems to check that they perform, as they should. Standards being developed include those for security and smart cards.

vi. *Cross-jurisdictional and societal aspects*: Standards are being developed to ensure that all legal and societal requirements involved in the use of biometrics are adequately met. The BioSec, CEN/ISSS, ISO/IEC and other groups are charged with developing technological standards, there is common agreement that success in biometrics deployments depend heavily on the willingness of people to use them. Standards need to be developed to ease such concerns as privacy, data protection, and health and safety issues, such as the ability to deduce the state of a person's health from biometric information.

The increased interest and advancing developments in biometrics have produced a necessity for the developments of standards to allow different systems to be compatible. The following standards are detailed in the Biometrics Resource Centre (2000) report:

i. *INCITS M1-Biometrics Technical Committee*: The Technical Committee M1, biometrics, has been established by the Executive Board of the International Committee for Information Technology Standards (INCITS) to ensure a high priority, focused, and comprehensive approach in the United States for the rapid development and approval of formal national and international generic biometric standards. Critical generic biometric standards include common file formats and application program interfaces. M1 has forty-two members from private industry, government agencies and academia. A first meeting Convener's report is available in the M1 Document Register.

ii. *Common Biometric Exchange File Format (CBEFF)*: The Common Biometric Exchange File Format (CBEFF) describes a set of data elements necessary to support biometric technologies in a common way independently of the application and the domain of use (e.g., mobile devices, smart cards, protection of digital data, biometric data storage). CBEFF facilitates biometric data interchange between different system components or between systems, promotes interoperability of biometric-based application programs and systems, provides forward compatibility for technology improvements, and simplifies the software and hardware integration process. CBEFF is being augmented under the NIST/BC Biometric Interoperability, Performance and Assurance Working Group to incorporate a compliant smart card format, Product ID, and a CBEFF nested structure definition.

iii. *BioAPI Specification (version 1.1)*: The BioAPI (version 1.1) defines an open system standard API that allows software applications to communicate with a broad range of biometric technologies in a common way. As an "open systems" specification, the BioAPI is intended for use across a broad spectrum of computing environments to ensure cross-platform support. It is beyond the scope of this specification to define security requirements for biometric applications and service providers, although some related information is included by way of explanation of how the API is intended to support good security practices. BioAPI V1.1 was developed by the BioAPI Consortium, which consists of eighty organisations representing biometric vendors, Original Equipment Manufacturers (OEMs), major Information Technology (IT) corporations, systems integrators, application developers, and end-users. BioAPI specifies standard functions and a biometric data format which is an instantiation of CBEFF.

iv. *Human Recognition Services module (HRS)*: The Human Recognition Services Module (HRS) is an extension of the Open Group's Common Data Security Architecture. CDSA is a set of layered security services and a cryptographic framework that provides the infrastructure for creating cross-platform, interoperable, security-enabled applications for client-server environments. The CDSA solutions cover all the essential components of security capability, to secure electronic commerce and other business applications with services that provide facilities for cryptography, certificate management, trust policy management, and key recovery. The biometric component of the CDSA's HRS is used in conjunction with other security modules (i.e., cryptographic, digital certificates, and data libraries) and is compatible with the BioAPI specification and CBEFF.

v. *American National Standards Institute (ANSI)*: The X9.F4 Working Group of American National Standards Institute (ANSI) Accredited Standards Committee X9 developed this American National Standards Institute (ANSI) standard, an ANSI accredited standards organisation that develops, establishes, publishes, maintains and promotes standards for the financial services industry. X9.84-2000 specifies the minimum-security requirements for effective management of biometrics data for the financial services industry and the security for the collection, distribution and processing of biometrics data. It specifies the following:

- The security of the physical hardware used throughout the biometric life cycle;

- The management of the biometric data across its life cycle;

- The utilisation of biometric technology for verification/identification of banking customers and employees;

- The application of biometric technology for physical and logical access controls;

- The encapsulation of biometric data

- Techniques for securely transmitting and storing biometric data.

The biometric data object specified in X9.84 is compatible with CBEFF.

vi. *ANSI/NIST-ITL 1-2000*: The ANSI standard specifies a common format to be used to exchange fingerprint, facial, scars mark and tattoo identification data effectively across jurisdictional lines or between dissimilar systems made by different manufacturers. On July 27, 2000, ANSI approved ANSI/NIST-ITL 1-2000. This is a revision, re-designation, and consolidation of ANSI/NIST-CSL 1-1993 and ANSI/NIST-ITL 1a-1997. NIST has published the document as NIST Special Publication SP 500-245. The revision began with a Fingerprint Data Interchange Workshop that was held in September 1998. This revision was performed in accordance with the ANSI procedures for the development of standards using the Canvass Method. All Federal, state and local law enforcement data is transmitted using the ANSI-NIST standard. This standard is a key component in allowing interoperability in the justice community (see Tables 1–4 and 1–11).

vii. *American Association for Motor Vehicle Administration (AAMVA)*: The American Association for Motor Vehicle Administration (AAMVA) Driver's License and Identification (DL/ID) Standard provide a uniform means to identify issuers and holders of driver license cards within the U.S. and Canada. The standard specifies identification information on drivers' license and ID card applications. In the high-capacity technologies such as bar codes, integrated circuit cards, and optical memory, the AAMVA standard employs international standard application coding to make additional applications possible on the same card. The standard specifies minimum requirements for presenting human-readable identification information including the format and data content of identification in the magnetic stripe, the bar code, integrated circuit cards, optical memories, and digital imaging. It also specifies a format for fingerprint minutiae data that would be readable across state and province boundaries for drivers' licenses. DL/ID-2000 is compatible with the BioAPI specification and CBEFF.

The British Standards Institution (BSI) began work on the standards in June 2004 and has published a set of four new BS ISO/IEC 19794 standards, covering the science of biometrics, using biological characteristics to identify individuals, according to reports. The standards are to ensure interoperability between the various products are inevitably come to market:

i. BS ISO/IEC 19784-2:2007 specifies the interface to an archive Biometric Function Provider. The interface assumes that the archive will be handled as a database, regardless of its physical realisation. (Smartcards, tokens, memory sticks, files on hard drives and any other kind of memory can be handled via an abstraction layer presenting a database interface.)

ii. BS ISO/IEC 19795-2:2006 provides requirements and recommendations on data collection, analysis and reporting specific to two primary types of evaluation: technology evaluation and scenario evaluation. It further specifies the requirements in the following areas:

- Development and full description of protocols for technology and scenario evaluations

- Execution and reporting of biometric evaluations reflective of the parameters associated with biometric evaluation types.

iii. BS ISO/IEC 24709-1:2007 defines a conformance testing methodology for ISO/IEC 19784-1. It specifies three conformance testing models that enable conformance testing of each of the following BioAPI components: an application, a framework and a BSP. It also specifies an assertion language that is used for the definition of test assertions. Actual test assertions for each of the BioAPI components are defined in subsequent parts of ISO/IEC 24709.

iv. BS ISO/IEC 24709-2:2007 defines a number of test assertions written in the assertion language specified in ISO/IEC 24709-1. These assertions enable a user to test the conformance to ISO/IEC 19784-1 (BioAPI 2.0) of any biometric service provider (BSP) that claims to be a conforming implementation of that International Standard.

The BS ISO/IEC 19794 series of standards cover the science of using biological properties to identify individuals and applies to access control and identification systems. The BS ISO/IEC 19794 standards are applicable to all identity management systems including:

- Identity document delivery and access management systems – such as border controls, corporate identity and access cards

- Prison access/egress

- Forensic identification – to identify casualties or suspects at the scene of a crime

- Citizens' rights – including voting, national health, unemployment benefits, driving licences

- Privileges associated with a particular employment category – including access to highly secure areas such as ports, airports, military establishments, company buildings, information systems

- Information stored on smart cards or other recognition tools, as well as the storage of biometric identification data in corporate databases.

- Recording of fingerprints, iris scans and facial recognition that is set to become a part of everyday access to services – including banking services, financial services, and online purchases.

Other biometrics standards that are resources for electronics professionals are briefly outlined in Table 1—11. The public and private sectors must conform to the international standards of using biometrics. Using the standards should ensure compatibility and interpretability. Biometric standards are in place to support the widespread adoption of biometrics. The industry is aware of the need and importance of standards and was very early to develop and promote them. Standards activities are expanding and the standards development efforts are accelerating to provide awareness and status of current standards and ongoing standards efforts. The range of biometric security access tools for PCs has been extended to mice and keyboards with integrated fingerprint scanners to web cam solutions whose software is able to recognise the facial features of registered persons to scanners that make use of the distinct iris patters of humans for identifying individuals. When the PC is booted the security software that goes with the tool writes itself into the log-on routine expanding the latter to include biometric authentication. In many instances the screen saver is integrated into the routine thus allowing for biometric authentication after breaks from work while the PC is still running. Sophisticated solutions, moreover, permit biometrically based security protection of specific programs and/or documents. The problem that all biometric security access procedures and devices still have in common are inability to establish fault tolerance limits.

Table 1–11. Selected biometrics standards

ANSI INCITS 383	Biometric Profile Interoperability and Data Interchange Biometrics-Based Verification and Identification of Transportation Workers information Technology
ANSI INCITS 394	Information Technology - Application Profile for Interoperability, Data Interchange and Data Integrity of Biometric-Based Personal Identification for Border Management

ANSI INCITS 395	Information Technology - Biometric Data Interchange Formats - Signature/Sign Data
ANSI INCITS 398	Information Technology - Common Biometric Exchange Formats Framework (CBEFF)
ANSI INCITS 409.1	Biometric Performance Testing and Reporting Part 1: Principles and Framework
ANSI INCITS 409.2	Biometric Performance Testing and Reporting Part 2: Technology Testing and Reporting
ANSI INCITS 409.3	Biometric Performance Testing and Reporting Part 3: Scenario Testing and Reporting
ANSI INCITS 409.4	Information Technology – Biometric Performance Testing and Reporting – Part 4: Operational Testing Methodologies
ANSI X9.84	Biometric Information Management and Security for the Financial Services Industry
BSI BS ISO/IEC 19784-1	Information Technology - Biometric application programming interface Part 1: BioAPI specification
BSI BS ISO/IEC 19785-1	Information Technology - Common Biometric Exchange Formats Framework Part 1: Data element specification
BSI BS ISO/IEC 19785-2	Information Technology - Common Biometric Exchange Formats Framework Part 2: Procedures for the operation of the Biometric Registration Authority
BSI BS ISO/IEC 19794-1	Information Technology - Biometric data interchange formats Part 1: Framework
BSI BS ISO/IEC 19794-3	Information Technology - Biometric data interchange formats Part 3: Finger pattern spectral data
BSI BS ISO/IEC 19794-4	Information Technology - Biometric data interchange formats Part 4: Finger image data
BSI BS ISO/IEC 19794-5	Information Technology - Biometric data interchange formats Part 5: Face image data
BSI BS ISO/IEC 19794-6	Information Technology - Biometric data interchange formats Part 6: Iris image data
CSA ISO/IEC 7816-11-05	Identification cards Integrated circuit cards Part 11: Personal verification through biometric methods-ISO/IEC 7816-11: 2004

Adopted from IHS Inc., (2005)

8. THE EUROPEAN COMMISSION

In 2005, the European Commission report on the effects of biometrics suggests that the use of biometrics can bring improved convenience and value to individuals. New legislation will probably be required to maintain security and privacy. It must also be recognised that biometrics have limitations, so it is impossible to achieve 100 per cent certainty. The biometric system should only form one part of an overall authentication or identification process. A number of recommendations have been put forward:

i.   The purpose of each biometric application must be clearly defined. Biometrics may challenge the trust between citizen and state by reducing the chances for privacy and anonymity.

ii. The use of biometrics must enhance privacy. The fears over invasion of privacy must be allayed. It is also possible for biometrics to enhance levels of privacy as they allow authentication without necessarily revealing a persons identity.

iii. To encourage the development of a vibrant European biometric industry. The large-scale introduction of biometrics opens up new technological areas in which European companies should be encouraged to participate.

iv. Fallback procedures should be established. Biometrics are not fully accurate or universally useable, so other systems should be put in place to cover this eventuality. These should be as secure and also must not stigmatise the user, e.g., people with unreadable fingerprints.

However, biometrics cannot be lost or stolen, but they can be copied. There are also problems with interoperability and international standards. The impact of multimodal biometrics needs to be assessed, since more than one biometric is to be incorporated in a high security environment and a full-scale field trial needs to be carried out to detect problems and assess the levels of costs. It would also be desirable for all EU states and participating countryies to adopt the same biometric technology (see chapter 5 for further discussion).

9.   SUMMARY OF CHAPTER ONE

This chapter has set the scene for the conceptual understanding of the key impacts of biometric security applications and types of biometrics. The direction to which this book is going has been made clear and the hypothesis has been postulated. The historical background of biometrics technologies has been established. The biometric devices are succeeding at an exponential rate with future advancements of accurate analysis and identification. Different types of biometric systems exist for identification and verification purposes but vary in prices, associated crossover error rates and user-acceptance levels.

It has already been established that biometrics technology are capable of decreasing costs and increasing convenience for both users and system administrators, but privacy and security of applications still remains questionable. There is no limit to where and when biometric devices could be used, as it may be installed for internal applications and infrastructure protection, such as for access control to sensitive spaces and computers. It will be necessary to carry out a cost benefit analysis to find out whether the use of biometrics will reduce for example, the amount of loss through fraud. The next chapter will exploits the biometrics measurements.

REFERENCES

Biometrics Resource Centre, 2000, *Biometric Standards and Current Standard-Related Activities*, http://www.itl.nist.gov/div893/biometrics/stand ards.html (February 21, 2007).

Campbell, P, Calvert, B and Boswell, S (2003) *Security guides to network security fundamentals*: Cisco learning institute.

Chirillo. S & Blaul. S, 2003, *Implementing Biometric Security*, John Wiley. Canada.

Desmarais, N., 2000, *Body language, security and E-commerce*, Library Hi Tech, 18(1):61–74.

Garfinkel, S., 2000, *Database Nation: The Death of Privacy in the 21st Century*, O'Rielly & Associates.

Hong, L., 1998, *Automatic personal identification using fingerprints*, PhD Thesis: Michigan State University.

Howarth F., 2000, *Standardisation Issues in Biometrics, Information security*, http://it-director. com/article.php?articleid=12568 (February 27, 2007).

IHS Inc., 2005, European Commission IDs Biometrics Challenges, The complete report is titled *Biometrics at the Frontiers: Assessing the Impact on Society*: Source —European Commission Directorate General Joint Research Centre (JRC), http://electronics.ihs.com /news/2005/ eu-biometrics-impact.htm (March 21, 2007)

Jain, A.K., Bolle, R., and Pankanti, S., 1999, *Personal Identification in Networked society*, Kluwer Academic Publisher.

Nalini, R.K., Senior, A., and Ruud, B.M., 1999, *Automated biometrics*; IBM Thomas J. Watson Research Centre Yorktown Heights, USA.

Ross, A.A., 2003, *Information fusion in fingerprint authentication*, PhD Thesis: Michigan State University.

Secguide, 2001, *Biometric Technologies*, http://www.secguide.com/edit orial_articles /biometric_technologies.htm (March 17, 2007).

Shoniregun, C. A., 2005, Impacts and Risk Assessment of Technology for Internet Security: Enable information Small-medium Enterprises (TEISMEs), Springer New York, USA.

Wayman, L, J., 2000, *National Biometric Test Centre collected works* (1997-2000), Version 1.2, San Jose State University, USA.

White, M., 2001, *Networking in a networked economy*, Finance on Windows, Summer,

Woodward D. John, Orlans M. Nicholas, Higgins T. Peter, 2003, *Biometrics: Identity Assurance in the Information Age*, Mc Graw Hill.

Zhang, D., Jing, X., and Yang, J., 2006, *Biometric image discrimination technologies*, Idea Group Inc publications, Hershey, USA.

Chapter 2

BIOMETRICS MEASUREMENTS

1.   INTRODUCTION

The biometric technologies measure a variety of anatomical, physiological and behavioural characteristics, to distinguish individual and to check that the image or signal presented is that of a real face, iris, fingerprint, palm and voice. Measurements of a living entity will vary and highly dependent on environmental conditions and user behaviour.

"Biometrics in a modern context is a highly relevant subject because of its applicability and scope on a global platform."

—International Association for Biometrics (iAfB) (2005)

The biblically documented biometric spoofing occurred when Jacob fooled his father Isaac into thinking that he is Esau his elder brother. The importance of a global focus on Biometrics are now addressed through the *International Association for Biometrics* (iAfB), a professional non-profit organisation, formed with the aim of providing a forum for the European and International Biometrics Community (EIBC) to be enlightened on the subject's intricacies. The iAfB offers facilitation to those interested to discuss themes relevant to biometrics, giving the impetus for personal opinions, share knowledge and information by participating in seminars, meetings, conferences and contributing articles. This chapter focuses on the biometrics measurements and also exploits their benefits and weaknesses.

2.   RELATED WORK

The success or failure of a biometric system in a particular application is not dependent upon the reliability of the biometric product alone. There are many other factors that contribute to the overall success or failure of a biometric, it is essential to understand that no single biometric technology offers a solution to all security problems, each biometric has its own strength and limitations, hence some biometric may be suitable for a particular authentication application (Jain *et al*, 2000). Modern biometric technologies provide enhanced security levels by introducing a new dimension in the authentication process called 'proof by property'. However, the design and deployment of a security architecture incorporating biometric technologies hides many pitfalls, which when underestimated can lead to major security weaknesses. Several factors determine the suitability of a particular biometric to a specific application; among these factors, the user acceptability seems to be the most significant. For many access control applications, like immigration, border control and dormitory meal plan access in prisons, very distinctive biometrics, e.g., fingerprint and iris, may not be acceptable for the sake of protecting an individual's privacy. In such situations, it is desirable that the given biometric indicator be only distinctive enough for verification but not for identification (Jain *et al*, 1997; and Ross, 2003). Among all biometric traits, fingerprints have one of the highest levels of reliability. Its uniqueness was discovered years ago, nonetheless the awareness was not until the late sixteenth century when the modern scientific fingerprint technique was first initiated. The English plant morphologist, Nehemiah Grew, published the first scientific paper report in 1684, that explained the ridge, furrow, and pore structure in fingerprints, as a result of his work, a large number of researchers followed suit and invested huge amounts of effort on fingerprint studies (Lee and Gaensslen, 2001).

In 1788, Mayer made a detailed description of the anatomical formations of fingerprints and fingerprint ridge characteristics were identified and characterised. Thomas Bewick in 1809 began to use his fingerprint as his trademark, which is believed to be one of the most important milestones in the scientific study of fingerprint recognition. In 1823 Purkinje, proposed the first fingerprint classification scheme, which classified fingerprints into nine categories according to the ridge configurations Henry Fauld, in 1880, first scientifically suggested the individuality of fingerprints based on an experimental observation. These findings established the foundation of modern fingerprint recognition. In 1899, Edward Henry established the well-known "Henry system" of fingerprint classification, made a significant advance in fingerprint recognition technology in 1899 (Moenssens, 1971; and Lee and Gaensslen, 2001)

In the early twentieth century, fingerprint recognition was formally accepted as a valid personal identification method and became a standard routine in forensics, various fingerprint recognition techniques, including latent fingerprint acquisition, fingerprint classification, and fingerprint matching were developed. With the rapid expansion of fingerprint recognition in forensics, operational fingerprint databases became so huge that it required a large amount of computational resources hence; manual fingerprint identification became infeasible (Hong, 1998). The FBI, UK Home Office, and Paris Police Department, in the early 1960s, began to invest a large amount of effort in developing automatic fingerprint identification systems (AFIS) (Lee and Gaensslen, 2001). Based on the observations of how human fingerprint experts perform fingerprint recognition, three major problems in designing AFISs were identified and investigated: digital fingerprint acquisition, local ridge characteristic extraction, and ridge characteristic pattern matching. Their efforts were so successful that today almost every law enforcement agency worldwide uses an AFIS. These systems have greatly improved the operational productivity of law enforcement agencies and reduced the cost of hiring and training human fingerprint experts. Automatic fingerprint recognition technology has now rapidly grown beyond forensic applications into civilian applications. In fact, fingerprint-based biometric systems are so popular that they have almost become the synonym for biometric systems. (Maltoni *et al*, 2003; Davies, 1994; and Hong, 1998). Forensic experts in criminal investigations have extensively used the fingerprint technologies for many years. The fingerprints are believed to be unique across individuals, and across fingers of the same individual. Even identical twins having similar DNA, are believed to have different fingerprints (Pankhanti *et al*, 2002; and Jain, 2002).

There are many privacy issues associated with transferring fingerprints over the network, because they reveal too much information about a person's identity (Jain *et al*, 2000). Fingerprint of a person does not change over time but, changes like minor cuts, bruises, for example farmers, or people that wash with hands or do any kind of work that will make their finger print ridges wear off may alter the structure of the finger print ridges. Moreover, the moisture content of the fingertip may change over time affecting the quality of the fingerprint image being acquired from a user. The template captured during enrolment will not capture these changes; therefore a protocol to update template data is necessary for system maintenance performance. Poor quality can also be provided by some users on a consistent basis perhaps due to the dry nature of their skin, therefore it is difficult to extract features from such poor quality images, so users providing such noisy finger print data will find it difficult to enrol in a biometric system that uses only finger prints, though the fingerprint can be enhanced but this can cause false ridges. So to address this issue, a multi-biometric system that uses other biometric traits is used in addition to fingerprint (Alonzo-Fernandez *et al*, 2005). Reports have shown that fingerprint technology has been subject to several attacks like spoofing where an imposter attempts to spoof biometric trait of a legitimate enrolled user in order to get round the system. It has been demonstrated that it is possible to construct artificial finger/prints in a reasonably amount of time to circumvent fingerprint authentication system. This type of attack is also common in signature and voice traits (for example the use of pictures, masks, voice recordings or speech synthesis tools can be used to deceive iris, face, and voice recognition systems). However, countermeasures must ensure that vitality detection features, which conduct an extra measurement of one or more attributes, such as the relative dielectric constant, the conductivity, the heartbeat, the temperature, the blood pressure, the detection of liveliness under the epidermis, or the spontaneous dilation and constriction of the pupil or eye movement, are integrated in the biometric system. If these features are not present, compensating controls such as the use of multi-biometrics must be applied (combination of face and lips movement recognition), or the implementation of interactive techniques (request for the user to say a specific phrase, or place 3 fingers in a certain order on the sensor) (Woodward *et al*, 2003).

Some of the limitations imposed by single biometric systems can be overcome by installing multiple sensors that capture different biometric traits. Such systems, known as multi-biometric systems, are expected to be more reliable due to the presence of multiple, independent pieces of evidence. These systems are also able to meet the stringent performance requirements imposed by various applications (Hong and Jain, 1998). Further, multi-biometric systems provide anti-spoofing measures by making it difficult for an intruder to spoof the multiple biometric traits of a genuine user simultaneously. By asking the user to present a random subset of biometric traits, the system can also ensure that a 'live' user is indeed present at the point of data acquisition. Multi-biometric systems have received much attention by associating different confidence measures with the individual biometric matchers. General strategies for combining multiple classifiers have been suggested by Hong *et al*, 1998. The integrate information presented by single or multiple biometric indicators can be use for three possible levels of fusion are:

i. Fusion at the feature extraction level obtained data from each sensor is used to compute a feature vector. As the features extracted from one biometric indicator are independent of those extracted from the other, it is reasonable to join the two vectors into a single new vector. The new feature vector now has a higher dimensionality and represents a person's identity in a different (and, hopefully, more discriminating) hyperspace. Feature reduction techniques may be employed to extract useful features from the larger set of features.

ii. Fusion at the matching score level provides a similarity score indicating the proximity of the input feature vector with the template vector. These scores can be combined to assert the veracity of the claimed identity. Techniques such as logistic regression may be used to combine the scores re-ported by the two sensors.

iii. Fusion at the decision level captures a biometric attribute and the resulting feature vectors are individually classified into the two classes –accept or reject. Fusion in the context of biometrics can take the following forms:

- Single biometric multiple representation.

- Single biometric multiple matchers.

- Multiple biometric fusions.

Overall performance is increased provided that the fusion scheme is adequately chosen (Garcia-Salicetti *et al.*, 2003; Ly Van *et al.*, 2003; and Sanderson *et al.*, 2003). In some cases, the two modalities that are combined may be correlated (for example lip movement and voice recorded together when a person is speaking, minimising the possibility of fraud). In such cases, it is interesting to fuse the information at an even earlier stage, namely just after feature extraction and to build a unique system taking as input a combination of these features (Brown *et al.*, 2002). Ross (2001), and Prabhakar and Jain (2002) observed the classifiers used for fusion have to be carefully selected in order to avoid performance degradation. A single Biometrics can also be matched severally using the same traits (e g finger print left loop, right loop, whorl can be matched, or a fingerprint biometric system may store multiple templates of a user's fingerprint (same finger) in its database. When a fingerprint impression is presented to the system for verification, it is compared against each of the templates, and the matching score generated by these multiple matches are integrated. Or a system may store a single template of a user's finger, but acquire multiple impressions of the finger during verification. Another possibility would be to acquire and use impressions of multiple fingers for every user that takes place in the matching stage of a biometric system, or it can be matched severally using different biometric traits, this seeks to improve speed and reliability of a biometric system.

Biometric Data can be captured from the communication channel (network), between the various point of the system, such as: the sensor and the feature extractor, the feature extractor and the matching algorithm or the matching algorithm and the application, in order to be replayed at another time for gaining access. This is also called electronic impersonation (or offline spoofing). This can be dealt with by the integration of the various parts of the system into a hardware security module, or generally the elimination of the transmission of the biometric template. A user usually leaves the residual biometric characteristic on the sensor either during enrolment or verification and this may be sufficient to allow access to an impostor (e.g. a fingerprint the sensor). The attack is realised by pressing a thin plastic bag of warm water on the sensor, by breathing on the sensor or by using dust with graphite, attaching a tape to the dust and pressing the sensor (Pankhanti *et al*, 2002). Even when a specific rule in the login algorithm is in place, for declining the exact same measurement, repositioning the tape to provide a slightly different input would deceive the system. A technology assessment should be conducted. The use of non-optical types of fingerprint sensors can counter this weakness or the use of liveliness as a measure can also counter the vulnerability. Imposters can continually attack a biometric system based on trial and error practices. The imposter continuously attempts to enter the system, by sending matching data to the system until a successful score is accomplished. This method is most effective in systems that implement identification rather than verification, since the biometric measurement is compared to a great number of templates, making the system weaker (as the number of users increases), due to the increased probability of the existence of similar templates this vulnerability can be countered by ensuring that controls such as the automatic locking of the user's account after a specific number of attempts, as well as the application of verification instead of identification if possible are in place (Woodward *et al*, 2003). It should be noted that the problem of automatic fingerprint matching has been extensively studied, nevertheless, the problem has not been fully resolved (Hong, 1998). Ross, 2003 reported that there is not much open literature addressing the research issues underlying hand geometry-based identity authentication; much of the literature is in the form of patents or application-oriented description. However, Woodward *et al*, 2003 stated that the largest application in use today is hand geometry at Disney world in Orlando, Florida.

The authentication of an individual identity is based on a set of hand features is an important research problem. It is well known fact that the individual hand features themselves are not very descriptive; devising methods to combine these non-salient individual features to attain robust positive identification is a challenging pattern recognition problem in its own right. Ross *et al*, 2003 and Woodward *et al*, 2003, reported that the system is not capable of capturing scars, ridges, or tattoos, though large rings, bandages and gloves can change the image and resultant measurement will be sufficiently different to cause a False rejection, more so, hands tend to be mirror images of one another, that it is possible to enrol with the right hand and use the left hand, turned upside down for verification, this can help in verification in case of injury on one of the hands.

The face recognition is one of the most active area of research with applications ranging from static, controlled mug shot verification to dynamic, uncontrolled face identification in a clustered background (Hong, 1998). Theoretically, it has the potential to become the most friendly and acceptable way to make personal identification (Newman, 1995), therefore people generally do not have any problem in accepting it as a feature. Substantial amount research has been devoted to face recognition in the past 25years (Jain *et al*, 2000). Research work in the field of face recognition brought about some proposed techniques such as principle component analysis (PCA), Linear Discriminate Analysis (LDA), singular value decomposition (SVD), local feature analysis, and a variety of neural network based techniques.

3.   BIOMETRIC METHODS

The ultimate form of electronic verification of physical attribute of a person to make a positive identification is biometrics. People have always used the brain's innate ability to recognise a familiar face and it has long been known that a person's fingerprints can be used for identification. The challenge has been to turn these into electronic processes that are inexpensive and easy to use. The main biometrics measurements are discussed below:

3.1   Hand geometry

Hand geometry involves the measurement and analysis of the hand shape. Though it is fairly simple to use and is very accurate compared to most biometrics. It requires special hardware and can be easily integrated into other devices. Unlike fingerprints, the hand is not unique because it can be distorted and features are not descriptive enough for identification. However, it is possible to devise a method by combining various individual palm features and measurements of fingers for verification purposes. The user is made to place the palm of his hand on a metal surface, which has guidance pegs on it. The palm and the hand are made up of ridges and furrows. The ridges are raised and the furrows are the lower portions. The difference between the ridges and the furrows creates enough space to enable the creation of patterns. The palm prints seem to be the future of authentication. The use of palm in biometrics is based on hand geometry structure. The metrics do not vary significantly across the population; they can nonetheless be used to verify the identity of an individual. Hand geometry measurement is non-intrusive and the verification involves a simple processing of the resulting features. The system computes 14 feature values comprising of the lengths of the fingers, widths of the fingers and the palm at various locations. Hand geometry information is not very distinctive (Ross, 2003, Hong, 1998).

Joseph Rice developed vein recognition in 1984, like fingerprints, the pattern of blood veins in the palm is unique to every individual, and apart from size, this pattern will not vary over the course of a person's lifetime (see Figure 2–1 for diagrammatic illustration).

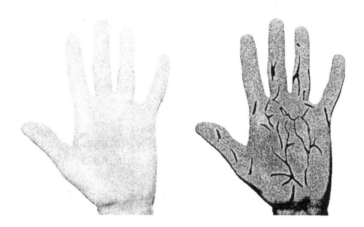

Figure 2–1. Hand and palm-vein pattern

The hand geometry scanner compares the shape of the user's hand to a template recorded during an enrolment session. If the template and the hand match, the scanner produces an output—which may serve as an authentication for unlocking a door, transmitting data to a computer, verifying or for identification, or log the person's arrival or departure times. During enrolment, which takes approximately 30 seconds, the user places the right hand in the reader three times. The unit's internal processor and software convert the hand image to a 9-byte mathematical template, which is the average of the three readings. The user's template may reside in internal memory (capable of holding over 27,000 users), or on other media such as a hard disk or smart card chip (see Figures 2–2 and 2–3 for diagrammatic illustrations). Hand geometry is a relatively accurate technology, but does not draw on as rich a data set as finger, face, or iris. A decent measure of the distinctiveness of a biometric technology is its ability to perform 1-to-many searches - that is, the ability to identify a user without the user first claiming an identity. Hand geometry does not perform 1-to-many identification, as similarities between hands are not uncommon. Where hand geometry does have an advantage is in its FTE (failure to enrol) rates, which measure the likelihood that a user is incapable of enrolling in the system. The hand biometrics technology aligns the hand so that the hand attributes can be read. This biometric system then checks its database for identification and verification of the user. The process usually takes less than 5 seconds (Huopio, 1998).

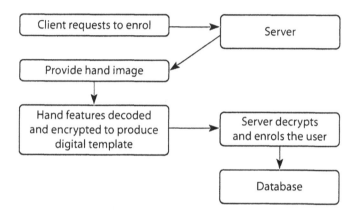

Figure 2–2. Hand recognition enrolment system

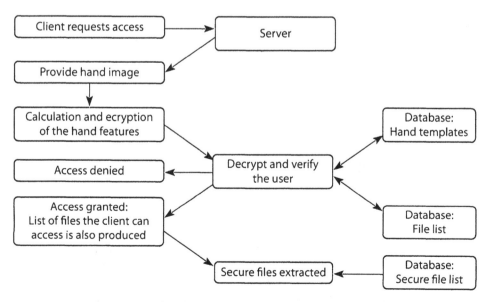

Figure 2–3. Access process for hand biometric

There has never been much improvement with hand biometrics technology apart from processors speed that has evolved over the past years. The benefits and weaknesses of the hand geometry are outline below:

i. Benefits

    •   Robust and reliable, it is not subjected to environmental conditions.

    •   The actual user interaction with a hand geometry scanner is quick and friendly.

    •   Requires low data storage – 20 bytes – so storing, searching and matching them can be done quickly even on low-end hardware.

    •   Convenient because one does not need to carry a card or memorise a PIN

    •   Resistant to fraud because it is impossible to submit a fake palm sample.

ii. Weaknesses

    •   Physically big to accommodate an entire human palm, the technology is usually the size of a toaster oven. This makes the equipment heavy and bulky; therefore it requires a large physical space.

    •   Higher level of false negatives and false positives than other types of biometrics. It has limited accuracy.

    •   Lack sanitary aspects. Putting the palm in the same place where thousands of other people have. Although, there are ways of keep the readers germ-free, but in this age of bird-flu panic, and many others transferable diseases, the concerns should not be lightly dismissed (Chirillo, and Blaul, 2003).

Furthermore, some hand geometry scanners do not have any way to detect whether a hand is living or not, therefore it can be fooled by a fake hand, if pressure is applied to the plate correctly and can recognised 30 images from the hand. Each human hand is unique. With different finger length, width, thickness, curvatures and relative location of these features are used to distinguish every human being from other .The hand geometry scanner uses a charge-coupled device (CCD) The process is much like placing a hand on a beaded projector screen. The hand scanner reads the hand shape by recording the silhouette of the hand. In combination with a side mirror and reflector, the optics produces two distinct images, one from the top and one from the side. This method is known as Orthographic scanning (Woodward *et al*, 2003).

3.2   Fingerprint scanning

The fingerprint technologies are the most advanced and commonly used biometrics technologies with very high accuracy. The challenges lie in the varying quality of fingerprints and the ability to deal with distortion, damage, irregularities ridges and valleys of one's finger. The new technologies have recently employed the use of pattern matching and ultrasonic scanning rather than evaluation of the irregularities, which has increased the accuracy of fingerprint scanning and reduced the risk of misidentification. By scanning the geometry of individual hands, taking into account the height, width, shape and proportion, the biometrics fingerprint technology can accurately recognise and identify individuals. This method is primarily used for physical access control and is considered the most useful in terms of durability and application. In fact, hand scanning is used effectively where other biometrics technologies cannot work due to frequency, volume, or environmental disruptions. The benefits and weaknesses of fingerprints are outline below:

i.   Benefits

• Very small storage space is required for the biometric template

• Allow access to multiple applications with, therefore there is no need to have multiple passwords.

• Track all accesses and control the system safely.

ii. Weaknesses

• The possibility to make a dummy, which will be accepted by the fingerprint scanner, makes the system weak with respect to some different attacks:

– A malicious person who wants to gain access inconspicuously intercepts a fingerprint from someone who is granted access. With this print, a dummy is created.

- – If a righteous person is willing to co-operate, one or several dummies can be created with which this individual can give access to whomever he wishes.

- – If a righteous person handles a transaction, he/she can claim to be framed by a malicious person. While the first two attacks on the system are possible with most verification systems, third claim can usually be disproved since the person making the claim must have revealed something. An example is fraud with a PIN protected credit card. If the fraud is committed using the PIN code, the probability that its owner has not been careful with the PIN is much higher than the probability that the PIN system is broken. But the fingerprint verification system is very susceptible to this attack since we all leave behind fingerprints everyday, everywhere without noticing it. Several scanner manufacturers claim to detect a living finger by detecting the heartbeat in the tip of the finger. This is possible, although some practical problems arise from this. People actively participating in a sport can have heart rhythm of less than forty beats per minute, meaning that they should keep their finger motionless on the sensor for at least four seconds for the rhythm to be detectable.

- • It has traditionally been associated with identifying and tracing criminal activities and thus users could be reluctant to adopt this form of biometric authentication

- • It is not 100 per cent unique to every user.

- • It lacks well-qualified optical system for an accurate recognition process.

- • Fingerprints duplication with co-operation (see brief discussion below).

- • Fingerprints Duplication without Co-operation (see brief discussion below).

3.2.1   Fingerprints duplication with co-operation

A wafer-thin silicon dummy can be created for a fingerprint if the owner of the fingerprint is willing to co-operate. This method requires only a limited amount of time (a few hours) and limited means (only cheap and easy accessible materials are used):

i. Beforehand, the finger should be washed with soap to make plaster flow more easily through the valleys of the print.

ii. Using modelling-wax a kind of saucer or bowl is formed at the nail side of the finger and around the tip of the finger (like a thimble with an opening where the actual fingerprint is). This bowl is filled with plaster to obtain a print of the finger. Preferably the plaster should be of a good quality (such as used by dental technicians or kits for creating plaster figures sold in hobby shops).

iii. In order to make a very thin dummy, a pounder that fits the mould can be created using plaster. The dried plaster is a bowl with a perfect fingerprint inside.

iv. Silicon waterproof cement (available in any do-it-yourself shop) or liquid silicon rubber is placed in the mould and the pounder is pressed firmly on top of this layer.

v. When the silicon has hardened, the dummy should be very carefully removed and is ready.

Another way to obtain a fingerprint could be the fingerprint scanner itself. Some more expertise is required to create a dummy from such a print, but every dental technician has the skills and equipment to create one.

3.2.2   Fingerprints duplication without co-operation

The duplication of a fingerprint without co-operation of its owner, a remake of a fingerprint that was left behind somewhere has to be made. The resulting dummy can of course be no better than the print itself, for a good dummy a good print is required:

i. First the print has to be copied from the material it is left on. The method used police can very easily be used for this. Visualisation of the print is done with a very fine powder put on the print with a brush. Some scotch tape is used to remove the powder from the underground.

ii. A camera and film are used to create a photo of the print by placing the tape on the photosensitive side of the film and making a picture of a diffuse light source.

iii. After developing the film, the negative is attached to a photosensitive printed circuit board (PCB). This is exposed to UV light after which the negative is removed and the PCB will be developed using an etching bath, the parts of the PCB that were exposed to the UV light are washed away. A final etching bath (sour) etches the copper layer. The result is a very slim profile (about 35 micron) that is an exact copy of print, copied in step 1.

vi. After deepening the profile to resemble the depth of a regular fingerprint, a silicon waterproof cement stamp can be created.

The fingerprint duplication with or without co-operation can be used to create an almost perfect copy of the finger in about eight hours, using materials that are available in do-it-yourself shops and electronics shops. The fingerprint is the oldest and the most widely use and recognised biometric pointer, they are based on taking a person's finger print's impressions (either using ink or a digital scan) and records its features (such as Whorls, arches, and loops are recorded along with the patterns of ridges, furrows, and minutiae) on the surfaces of the hand. This information is then processed or stored as an image or as an encoded computer algorithm in a data base to be compared with other fingerprint records during verification this is done by the user pressing his finger gently against a small reader surface (optical or silicon) usually of about 2 inch square. The reader is attached to a computer, which takes the information from the scan, and sends it to the database. There it is compared to the information within. The user is usually required to leave his finger on the reader for less than 5 seconds during which time the identification or verification takes place. Presently, many systems check for blood flow, or check for correctly arrayed ridges at the edges of the fingers. This is done to prevent fake fingers from being used. The fingerprint application has been in existence since the 14th century and one of the most widely use biometric application. The fingerprints are used as personal marks or signatures in parts of Asia. Dr Faulds, while serving in Japan in 1870s as a missionary doctor, uncovered ancient fingerprint impressions embedded on pottery shards found in shell pits. He determined that the impression were the distinctive marks of the artist, thus inspired he started work on fingerprints, he collected finger prints of infants to check if their fingerprints will change as they grow. His research demonstrated that it is possible to match a latent, or partial fingerprint left at a crime scene with a person, his work helped to bring about a major break through in the area of crime investigation. The storing of fingerprint information has changed and images are stored as an algorithm, so that it is not easily readable. The fingerprint ridges are formed between the third and fourth month of faetal development. The ridges start to develop on the skin of the thumbs and fingers. The ridges give a firmer grasp to avoid slippage (allowing the fingers to grasp and pick up objects). All fingerprints have a unique combination of patterns and ridge characteristics. The patterns of the ridges contain rows of sweat pores that allow sweat and or oil to exit from glands. The sweat that mixed with other body oils and dirt produces fingerprints on smooth surfaces. The three main types of fingerprints are briefly discuss below:

i. The *visible prints* or the *patent prints* are left in some mediums. The common example is when blood, dirt, ink or grease on the finger come into contact with a smooth surface and leave a friction ridge impression that is visible without development.

ii. The *latent prints* are not visible. They are formed by the sebaceous glands on the body or water, salt, amino acids and oils contained in sweat. The sweat and fluids create prints that are processed before they can be seen or photographed. The latent prints can be visible by dusting, fuming or chemical reagents.

iii. The *impressed prints* or plastic prints are indentations left in soft pliable surfaces (clay, wax, paint…) that will take the impression. The impressed prints are visible and can be viewed or photographed without been processed.

The fingerprint patterns are divided into three main groups: arches, loops and whorls. Many research works has been published to proved the accuracy of the fingerprints and it has been established that approximately five percent of all fingerprints are Arches, 30% are Whorls and 65% are Loops (see Figure 2–4 for patterns representation).

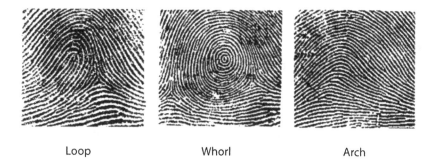

Loop   Whorl   Arch

Figure 2–4. Fingerprint patterns

While most manufacturers use minutiae, about 20% use pattern matching, which extrapolates information from a number of ridges, but this requires the same section of ridge patterns in a specific part of the fingerprint to be detected each time it is used. If multiple ridges are used it reduces the need for minutiae points to be detected. The templates for measuring ridge patterns are about three times larger {900-1200 bytes} than the templates needed for minutiae data. The three main types of fingerprint scanners are discussed below:

i. *Optical scanners.* These are the oldest and most proven technology. They are capable of withstanding wide temperature fluctuations, are inexpensive to produce and provide a resolution up 500 dpi. The finger is placed on glass plate and then scanned using an array of light emitting diodes to illuminate the valleys and ridges of the fingerprint. The optical scanners use a charge coupled device (CCD), to produce a picture of the fingerprint, each diode in the CCD produces one pixel of information. The dark ridges and the light valleys are converted into a digital signature. Each pixel is then combined to produce the final usable image, which is checked for quality, e.g., to light or dark, or a low image definition. To give a usable image automatic adjustments are made, if necessary manual adjustments can be made, but this is a difficult procedure. If the image is not of a high enough quality another is taken. Problems are encountered due to their size, since the plate has to be sufficiently large enough to produce a quality image. Problems have also been encountered with latent prints from previous users, which reduce the clarity of the image produced. They are relatively small, inexpensive devices that are easily incorporated into, or connected to most personal computers.

ii. *Silicon scanners,* also known as capacitance scanners. These scanners utilises chip technology based on DC capacitance, have increased their market share in recent years since first being developed in the late 1990's. The touch sensitive chips are a newer technology that allows for even smaller unit design. The finger acts as one plate of the capacitor and the silicon sensor acts as the other. They are composed of a silicon plate containing a large number of small capacitors in a matrix. The capacitance between the finger and the plate is converted into an 8-bit greyscale digital image. They use an electrical current to get the image, with the capacitance varying depending on how far the current has too travel, therefore a valley will produce a different capacitance from a ridge. The chips consist of rows and columns of about 200 to 300 lines in a chip measuring 1 by 1.5 cm that produce high quality images. The silicon sensors are small enough to be incorporated into many peripheral devices such as mobile phones mouse and keyboards. The silicon is covered in a hard resistant protective coating, which must be as thin as possible to allow contact with the finger to be as close as possible (Technews, 2005). Research is continuing to make the surfaces more durable, with some manufacturers claiming durability 100 times better than is obtained with optical scanners. Capacitance scanners tend to be more accurate than optical scanners, and since they use a computer chip instead of a CCD they can be made more compact than optical devices. As research and development has continued both the size and the cost of producing the chip have been reduced.

iii. *Ultrasonic sensors.* These are the newest technology and hence the least common type in use. They are also regarded as the most accurate. The scanners work by transmitting ultrasonic waves to measure the distance based on the impedance of the finger the plate and the air. It is capable of penetrating dirt and residue on the surface of he skin and the plate. Early research suggests that ultrasonic sensors combine the advantage of larger plate size and ease of use of optical scanners with the ability of silicon scanners to overcome poor reading conditions.

The scanners use complex algorithms to recognise the minutiae and measure their relative positions. To find a match between two prints all the minutiae do not need to be found, the sensitivity of the system varies according to how it has been programmed. The intelligent agent in biometrics devices are able to differentiate and recognised the fingerprint patterns of the user based on the most common line-types found in prints:

* *Rod* forms a straight line. It has no re-curve features and tends to be found in the centre of the fingerprint's pattern area.

* *Ellipse* is a circular or oval shaped line-type, which is generally found in the centre of Whorl patterns.

* *Spiral* line-type is generally found in whorl print patterns and spirals out from the centre of the fingerprint.

* *Bifurcation* is the intersection of two or more line-types that converge or diverge.

* *Tented arch* resembles the tent. The line-type rises and falls at a steep.

* *Loop* is a re-curve line-type. It enters and leaves from the same side of the fingerprint.

- *Island* is a line-type that stands alone and totally contained in the pattern area of interest.

- *Sweat gland* contains many sweat glands. The moisture and oils allows the fingerprint to be electronically imaged.

- *Minutiae points* are common micro features in a fingerprint. They are the intersection of bifurcations, ending points of Islands and the centre point of the sweat glands.

- *Arch* can be found in most print patterns. The fingerprints that make up the Arches are sometimes classified as Arch prints.

The fingerprints cannot be altered without creating a new unique fingerprint. Even when the skin tissue is injured or dirty/worn down from abrasion or with rare skin diseases the skin that grows back will have the same print. The prints remain the same throughout life. The print that someone is born with does not change during the life time. For many years, law enforcement agencies have used automated fingerprint matching devices. Increasingly, smart cards, which include biometric information such as fingerprints, are being used to improve security at borders and at federal facilities. The increased use and the desire to limit storage space needed on these cards is driving the use of minutiae rather than full images. A study by the National Institute of Standards and Technology (NIST) shows that computerised systems that match fingerprints using interoperable minutiae templates mathematical representations of a fingerprint image can be highly accurate as an alternative to the full fingerprint image. NIST conducted the study, called the Minutiae Interoperability Exchange Test (MINEX), to determine whether fingerprint system vendors could successfully use a recently approved (InterNational Committee for Information Technology Standards-378) for minutiae data rather than images of actual prints as the medium for exchanging data between different fingerprint matching systems. The U.S. Departments of Homeland Security and Justice sponsored the MINEX. The minutiae templates are a fraction of the size of fingerprint images require less storage memory and can be transmitted electronically faster than images. However, the techniques used by vendors to convert fingerprint images to minutiae are generally proprietary and their systems do not work with each other. Fourteen fingerprint vendors from around the world participated in MINEX. Performance depended largely on how many fingerprints from an individual were being matched. Systems using two index fingers were accurate more than 98 percent of the time. For single-index finger matching, the systems produced more accurate results with images than with standard minutia templates. However, systems using images and two fingers have the highest rates of accuracy of 99.8 percent (B & J Biometrics, Inc., 2006).

3.3   Facial scanning

The facial identification is probably the most common biometric characteristic used by human to make a personal identification and involves extracting a feature set from a two-dimensional image of the user's face and matching it with the template stored in the database. The feature extraction process is often preceded by a face detection process during which the location and spatial extent of the face is determined.

The face is an important part of human body and how people can identify a person. Imagine how hard it would be to recognise an individual if all faces looked the same. The face is arguably a person's most unique physical characteristic and humans have had the innate ability to recognise and distinguish different faces for millions of years, computers are just now catching up. The facial recognition is based on the ability to first recognise faces, which is a technological fit in itself, and then measure the various features of each face. It may be far too soon to call the facial biometrics industry 'mature'. Jain and Bolle (1999), proposition of six universal expressions would be adopted. The six universal recognised expressions are happy, sad, disgust, fear, surprise and

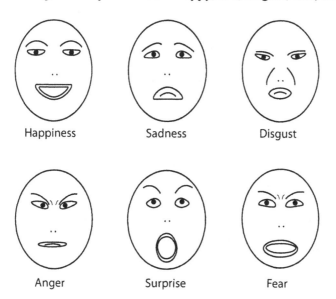

Figure 2–5. Six universal expressions

anger in comparison with the neutral face (see Figures 2–5 and 2–6 for diagrammatical illustration).

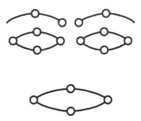

Figure 2–6. Distance transform

The eyes and nose tip are estimated by visualising the fact that nose tip and centre of both eyes form equilateral triangle. So the eye middle points are estimated and the height is calculated by using formula (see Equation 2–1).

Therefore 'α' is the length of side.

$$h = \alpha \sin 60° = \frac{1}{2}\sqrt{3}\alpha \qquad (2\text{–}1)$$

The control points are required for analysis: eyebrow, eye, middle point of upper, lower eyelid and two extreme corners of eye, four lip control points which are left, right, top and bottom control points of lips (see Figure 2–6 for diagrammatical illustration). The distances d is the Euclidean distances in the control points with reference to neutral face (see Equation 2–2).

$$d = \sqrt{(x_2 - x_1)^2 + (y_2 - y_1)^2} \qquad (2\text{–}2)$$

The ratio of eyes and lips in gestured image are calculated and its difference with the ratio of eyes and lips of neutral image. Statistical analysis of these distances classifies the gestured image into the corresponding expression. The ability of a computer to detect, analyse and recognised the user's face has many applications in human-computer interaction (HCI), so the automated analysis of faces showing different expressions has been studied to improve mapping quality of user's biometric profile.

The facial scanning applications are most often used in conjunction with other verification methods such as identification cards systems or with existing security cameras and monitors. This method utilises high-resolution images of distinct facial features such as eye sockets, shape of the nose, and/or the position of certain features relative to each other. Problems arise with this application if the subject is not properly positioned for the camera or environmental changes (as lighting can prevent an accurate read). The benefits and weaknesses of facial identification are outline below:

i. Benefits

- The acquisition data are non-intrusive

ii. Weaknesses

- User must position face in same position at all time for the scan because facial expressions could cause false rejects.

- Lighting is very important for accurate verification.

- Violation of privacy as data may be captured for verification without

- user's knowledge.

- Twins can be falsely identified.

- Environmental conditions, such as extreme heat or cold, can affect thermal facial scan technologies.

- Hair changes can cause false rejects.

- Facial hair growth and aging can cause false rejects.

- Glasses can alter a user's ability to be recognised if they are removed or added after enrolment.

- Distance variation can lead to false rejects and prevent unique information from being acquired during the enrolment process.

- Lack considered as secure as some other biometric technologies such as fingerprint, iris or retinal.

- Can be easily tricked or faked.

There is new software, which can recognise faces within a crowd in the attempt to match them to stored images of known criminals. With the recent terrorist attacks there has been a tremendous push to implement this technology in a variety of public places such as airports, government buildings, border crossings, and other vulnerable areas. The facial recognition is the most natural means of biometric identification. The method of distinguishing one individual from another is an ability of every human being. The face of a person is considered to be the most immediate and transparent biometric modality for physical authentication applications. The problem of recognising people from their facial images has gained wide attention. For visible spectrum imaging, there have been many studies reported in the literature. Research in facial recognition has shown that the variation in facial imaging due to illumination is greater than the variation in identity cards.

3.4   Iris scanning

The iris patterns for personal identification were originally proposed in 1936 by ophthalmologist Frank Burch. By the 1980's the idea had appeared in James Bond films, but it still remained science fiction and conjecture. In 1987 two other ophthalmologists, Aran Safir and Leonard Flom, patented this idea, and in 1989 they asked John Daugman at Harvard University, to try to create the actual algorithms for iris recognition. These algorithms, which Daugman patented in 1994 and are owned by Iridian Technologies, are the basis for all current iris recognition systems and products.

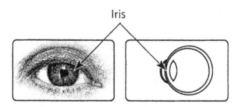

Figure 2–7. Understanding iris recognition

The eyeglasses and contact lenses present no problems to the quality of the image and the iris-scan systems test for a live eye by checking for the normal continuous fluctuation in pupil size. The inner edge of the iris is located by an iris-scan algorithm, which maps the distinct patterns and characteristics of the iris. An algorithm is a series of directives that tell a biometric system how to interpret a specific problem. The algorithms have a number of steps and are used by the biometric system to determine if a biometric sample and record is a match (see Figure 2–7 for diagrammatical illustration). The iris features consists of the coloured tissue surrounding the pupil which has more than 200 points that can be used for comparison, including rings, furrows and freckles. It has the ability to create an accurate measurement that can be used for identification purposes, and not just verification. The uniqueness of eyes, even between the left and right eye of the same person, makes iris scanning very powerful for identification purposes. Its relative speed and ease of use make it a great potential biometric. It also takes up a bit more memory for the data to be stored, but with the advances in technology, this is unlikely to cause any major difficulty. The Iris-scan technology has been piloted in the UK, US, Japan and Germany since as early as 1997. This entails a camera acquiring the eye image of a user and processes it to locate the iris, and compute the Iris code when the user looks into the biometric camera. The computed iris code is compared with the data residing in the database to complete user verification. Iris is unique for every individual and it never changes during the person's lifetime, an impostor cannot get feature because it is internal, and therefore almost impossible to copy. The iris-scan technology is used for people working in high-security areas.

In these pilots the customer's iris data became the verification tool for access to the bank account, thereby eliminating the need for the customer to enter a PIN number or password. When the customer presented their eyeball to the automated teller machine (ATM) machine and the identity verification was positive, access was allowed to the bank account. These applications were very successful, eliminated the concern over forgotten or stolen passwords, and received tremendously high customer approval ratings. Many Airports have begun to use iris-scanning for such diverse functions as employee identification/verification for movement through secure areas and allowing registered frequent airline passengers a system that enables fast and easy identity verification in order to expedite their path through passport control. The false acceptance rate for iris recognition systems is 1 in 1.2 million, statistically better than the average fingerprint recognition system. However, a downside of iris-scan technology is that it is still not accepted as a proven technology and its validity has not yet been established. Also many people are very sceptical of the iris-scan and always protective of their eyes. The iris recognition provides real-time, high-confidence recognition of a person's identity through mathematical analysis of random patterns in the iris. Irises (pigmented, round, contractile membranes in the eyes) are unique in each individual. The iris is a protected internal organ whose random texture is stable and unchanging, from about one year of age until death. It is the most individually distinctive feature of the human body. No two irises are alike, not even among twins. In fact, left and right irises of one individual are not identical. The iris scanning is similar to retinal scanning with level of accuracy. Its application is considered less intrusive and is thus becoming more common. The iris scanning is mostly used in government department, airports, and banks, but the system integration remains a challenging part of implementation and improvements are continually being made. The benefits and weaknesses of iris identification are outline below:

i. Benefits

   • Non-intrusive, camera can be at a distance of 12 ft.

   • Very accurate in identifying users.

   • Requires low data storage for template.

ii. Weaknesses

   • Low user acceptance rate.

   • Very expensive.

   • Required special hardware.

The iris recognition is forecast to play a role in a wide range of other applications in which a person's identity must be established or confirmed. These include electronic commerce, information security, and entitlements authorisation, building entry, automobile ignition, forensic and police applications, network access and computer applications. It appears to be the most secure possible way of controlling entry to premises.

However, the speed and accuracy of iris coding has led to a number of commercial iris recognition products. Iris codes provide the lowest false accept rates of any known verification system zero, in tests conducted by the U.S. Department of Energy. The equal error rate has been shown to be better than one in a million, and if one is prepared to tolerate a false reject rate of one in ten thousand, then the theoretical false accept rate would be less than one in a trillion. The main practical problem facing deployment of iris scanning is getting the picture without being too intrusive. The iris is small (less than half an inch) and an image including several hundred pixels of iris is needed. There is no technical reason why a camera could not acquire the iris from a distance of several feet given automatic facial feature recognition.

3.5   Retinal scanning

The retina is the light receptive area at the back of the eye on which the image is focused and made up of light receptors with complex network of blood vessels. The pattern of the blood vessels is unique even between identical twins and is also very stable since it can only be altered by a small number of diseases or serious physical injury. The retinal scanning is considered to be the most accurate of all the biometric technologies through its evaluation of the shape and make-up. It is a fairly costly technology and often perceived as difficult to use. Other complications include interference from foreign objects such as eyeglasses or contact lenses. Even so, the accuracy of retinal scanning and the minimal risk of imitation make it useful in extremely high security areas where accountability is of utmost importance. The benefits and weaknesses of retinal scanning are outline below:

i. Benefits

  • Highly accurate in identifying users.

  • Requires low data storage for templates.

ii. Weaknesses

  • Low user acceptance rate.

  • Very expensive.

  • Required special hardware.

  • Difficult to use.

The retina scanner scans the unique patterns of the blood vessels at the back of the eye on the retina using a low intensity light source via an optical coupler. One example of a retinal scanner is the 'EyeDentity' system which uses infrared light to perform a 360 degree scan of the back of the eye to get the retinal scan and map the vascular pattern. The camera records 192 data points, and the total eye signature requires 96 bytes of memory storage (see Figure 2–8 for diagrammatic illustration).

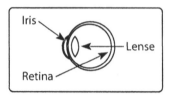

Figure 2–8. Retina recognition

As with all biometric systems the first stage is enrolment, when the user's retinal pattern is taken, measured and stored in the database. In verification the retinal scan is compared with previous authorised scans held on the database. The time taken to search the database varies from 3 seconds for a database of 4000 images up to 15 seconds for a database of 3,000,000 images. The sensor can be either linked to a central database controlling a number of scanners, or they can operate as stand alone units, which are capable of storing up to 3,500 images. The system has been in use by FBI, CIA and NASA. So far the system has only been used for access control, but future applications are time attendance, computer database security, issuing documents such as driver's licences, benefits payments, patient control, voter registration, ATM's and credit card authentication (Womack, 1994) A company called 'Retica' produces a scanner, which uses LED and CCD technology to record an image of the retina (Retica Systems 2005). The data is then stored and compared against a database. The company also produces a dual scanner which simultaneously records retina and iris patterns, which are then combined to produce iris and retina data that can be cross correlated to improve the accuracy of the identification. It has been proved to be an accurate technology, but it does involve the user looking into a receptacle and focusing on a given point. There are problems with user acceptance with it being inconvenient for those who wear glasses and those who avoid intimate contact with the receptacle (Biometrics Consortium, 2005). Retinal scanners can only realistically be deployed in high security areas, where they are likely to become more common.

3.6   Voice authentication

The voice authentication recognised the user's particular word or phrase. The voice scanners can have a problem with false non-matching, failing to authenticate a known user, but they tend to be resistant to false matching, so impostors are unlikely to be authenticated.

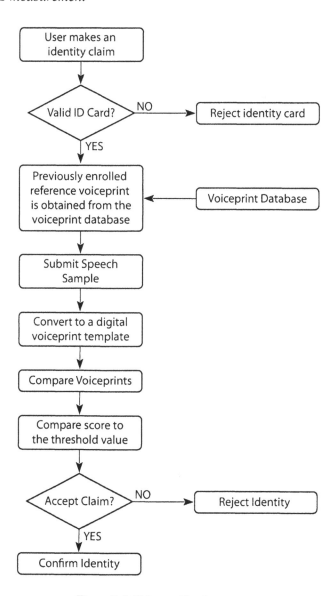

Figure 2–9. Voice verification process

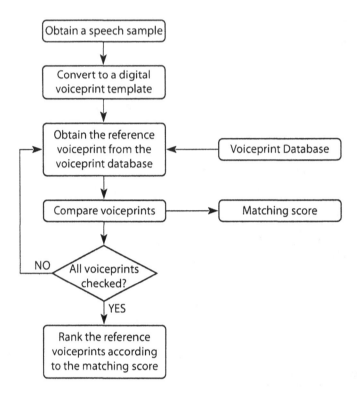

Figure 2–10. Voice identification system

Voice biometrics are a numerical model of the sound, pattern and rhythm of an individual's voice. A voice biometric or 'voice print' is unique to an individual. A flow chat of voice verification recognition and identification process is presented in Figures 2–9 and 2–10. As long as a voice channel is established during an authentication session, applying voice biometric authentication for even higher levels of authentication and security can be added to authentify application. The following applications can be incorporated with voice biometrics:

- Voice Authenticated Password Reset

- e-signature

- Transaction Authorisation

- B2B Transactions

- Secure Information Access

- Digital Credential Distribution

The scanning systems measure both behavioural and physiological elements of the individual's speech including what has been said and how the word or phrase is spoken, that comprises of the pattern. This version of biometric scanning is popular as it is quick and easy to use. However, the accuracy of feature can be faulted if the user's voice is distorted due to sickness or by environmental interruptions. The benefits and weaknesses of voice authentication are outline below:

i. Benefits

- Non-intrusive. Users are always will to use voice authentication.

- The hardware is very cheap and readily available (Microphone)

ii. Weaknesses

- Background noise affects the quality and accuracy of the result.

- The templates tend to be very large; five to ten times the size of a fingerprint template and requires large storage space between 2,000 and 10,000 bytes.

- It can be easily influenced by extraneous circumstances. For example sore throat, common cold, or weather condition.

- Remote access phone lines may produce poor transmission.

- Poor quality of transmitted voice traits.

The voice recognition allows the user to use their own voice as an input device; it can be used to dictate text or to give commands such as a password to a computer. The voice scanner measures specific features of the voice pattern, which is then used to produce a voice template, to be used for authentication. In enrolment an individual is prompted to select a pass-phrase or a sequence of numbers.

3.7   Signature scanning

The signature scanning involves the evaluation of both the signature and the behavioural characteristics (pressure, speed, and type of stroke). The use of behavioural characteristics prevents counterfeit signatures and makes this biometric method highly accurate. The reliability is consideration when the individual changes his or her signature or method of writing. The handwritten signature is a biometric property. The signature is a long-standing method in verification, but it does have a problem in being easy to forge visually, but it is more difficult to forge the behaviour of the user while writing the signature. Signatures are unique to an individual and they do tend to vary slightly each time they are written. These variations make signature verification a difficult pattern recognition problem. The signature verification can be done offline or online. Offline signature verification or simple verification requires the signature on the document to be scanned to obtain its digital image representation; a comparison of appearance only is then made. Online signature verification or dynamic verification, in that it measures how the signature was made, making it more secure and therefore more complex; it requires special hardware, e.g., a digitising tablet or a pressure sensitive pen which records the movements of the pen. Online signature verification also allows the dynamics of writing to be captured, such as speed, pressure, acceleration, deceleration and the amount of time the pen spends in contact with the paper, which is not available through the two dimensional offline verification methods. This biometric measure can be used to check signatures on documents, cheques etc, and in the future you may be able to sign into your computer instead of using a password. The signature is harder to steal or guess than a password, and is easier for the user to remember (Jain *et al.*, 2002). The biometric signatures should not be confused with digital signatures. A digital signature is a long numerical code that has been uniquely assigned to a person; it has nothing to do with a real signature. A certificate of authority is use by digital signature and biometric signature is recorded using an input device, which allows hand written signatures to be incorporated into e-documents during electronic transactions. The main consumers for signature verification biometrics are currently in the finance sector, such as banks and insurance companies.

3.8   Keystroke dynamics

The keystroke dynamics is purely a behavioural biometric, in that it detects the rhythm with which the user types out a message on the keyboard. It is often used in conjunction with a password, to detect whether the user or somebody else is trying to type in the password. The keyboard functions as the acquisition device, the operating system can measure how long each key is depressed and the time between keystrokes. This data is gathered by keystroke scanning systems and a distinctive set of characteristics is recorded. Enrolment can be inconvenient since the username and password must be a minimum length and needs to be typed approximately 15 times to produce the enrolment template. Keystroke scans will not work if the user makes a mistake when typing the password; the whole word needs to be typed correctly. The templates generated by keystroke scanners store the behavioural data such as speed and rhythm, alongside the username and password data. The distinctive features of touch typing are likely to be stronger in those who are more experienced, but these typists may have less distinctive typing styles than less experienced typists. To provide enough data to confirm the rhythm of typing the passwords should have a minimum length, which will depend on the chosen system and the requirements of the systems administrator. The degree of correlation between the enrolment and verification templates is adjusted accordingly, as the level of security is increased or decreased (Nanavati, and Thieme, 2002).

A system from a company called 'bio password', uses a software program which captures the unique keystroke pattern of the user, which combined with a password produces what has been termed a 'hardened password' which is more difficult to compromise. The system also utilises the existing keyboard so can be cheaply incorporated into existing operations. The major advantage of keystroke dynamics is that it is low cost and can be easily deployed into large-scale operations. Further research needs to be carried out to determine just how accurate keystroke dynamics are. At high security settings problems have been encountered with users being rejected and it is also still possible that unauthorised users may be allowed access. It is only viable to use this method for low security operations, preferably in conjunction with passwords. These passwords can also be changed easily and should be changed frequently.

3.9   Ear shape recognition

It has been suggested that the shape of the ear and the structure of the cartilaginous tissue of the pinna are distinctive. Matching the distance of salient points on the pinna from a landmark location of the ear is the suggested method of recognition in this case. This method is not believed to be very distinctive.

3.10   Odour recognition

The odour recognition has been an area of interest to many researchers, with a significant recognition to the work of Li and Hopfield (1989) Erdi and Barna (1991), and Nakamoto, *et al.*, (2001). More recently, Temel and Karlik (2007) explained the high-performance biologically inspired odour identification system. The smell sensory system has not been well understood yet. However, it is known that formation of smell is first subject to excitation, which needs to reach the olfactory region with airflow. In normal respiration, main airflow does not reach this region. The smell is sensed with particular diffusion. During sniff, which may be intentional or spontaneous response to odour stimuli, and changes on vestibule, the airflow becomes stronger and it is directed at olfactory region (Nakamoto *et al.*, 2001). The spatio-temporal codes generated by sensing cells are converted to neural pulses, which will then be imaged to certain critical areas in brain (see Figure 2–11 for diagrammatical illustration).

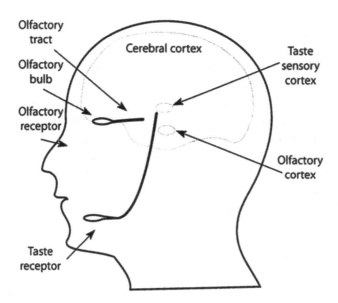

Figure 2–11. The functional units of the brain

The Figure 2–11 illustrates the functional units of the brain (major processes in the olfactory system) entitled to information processing. The olfactory cortex performs pattern classification and recognition of the odours sensed. Identified odour information is conveyed to hippocampus, limbic system, and the cerebral cortex. The subconscious memory evoke of odour can be accounted for by the connection to the hippocampus. Conscious perception of the odour and how to act on the odour takes place in the cerebral cortex (Li and Hopfield, 1989). The mammalian olfactory system uses numerous chemical sensors; olfactory receptors combined with signal processing in the olfactory bulb and automated pattern recognition in the olfactory cortex of the brain. Sensing an odour begins at nasal mucosa composed of olfactory and respiratory regions. Olfactory region is corresponds to upper nasal cavity, superior on turbinal region and almost occupy 1/3 of the upper nasal septum. A human has almost 50 million receptive olfactory cells. Olfactory cells are bipolar resident cells amongst supportive cells. Each cell has a sensorial receptor and periphery extension neuron. On the surface of an olfactory cell are cilia with lipid contents therefore substances that are concentrated at extension of odour cells are better sensed by reaching bulbus olfactory passing through the lamina cribrosa forming olfactory.

The artificial nose has been developed to automatically sense/detect and classifies odours, vapors, and gases (Érdi and Barna, 1991; Nakamoto, 2001). The two important operations performed by an electronic nose are the sensing of odours and automated recognition of pattern ensembles. The sensing system can be an array of several sensing elements, e.g. chemical sensors where each element measures a different property of the sensed odour, or it can be a combination. Each odour presented to the sensor array produces a signature or pattern characteristic of the odour, hence producing a database of signatures is built up. This database of labelled odour signatures is used to train the pattern recognition system. The goal of this training process is to configure the recognition system to produce unique mappings of each odour so that an automated identification can be performed (Baby *et al.*, 2000 and Bourgeois and Stuetz, 2000).

In order to increase the performance of the pattern recognition, input samples can be further pre-processed (see Figure 2–12 for diagrammatical illustration). Linear Discriminant Analysis (LDA) by McLachlan (1992) has been widely used for enhancing the data separation ability as well as feature extraction (see Equation 2–3). This method takes into account not only the within-class scatter but also between-class scatters, leading to a highly effective solution to many pattern classification problems. In a multi-class case, as a generalisation to Fisher discriminant, consider the transformation on input vector x:

$$y = Ax \qquad (2\text{--}3)$$

Figure 2–12. A neural-network with input pre-processing

Optimum class separation can be obtained by maximising the objective function (Bourgeois and Stuetz, 2000):

$$J(A) = Tr\left\{ \left(A\Delta_w A^T \right)^{-1} \left(A\Delta_B A^T \right) \right\}$$
(2–4)

Where '*Tr*' denotes the trace of a matrix, '*T*' is the transpose; Δ_W and Δ_B are the total within-class and the between-class covariance matrices, respectively. It should be noted that those definitions are valid in original x space. The complete solution to above optimisation problem involves a utilisation of spectral (eigen) decomposition, which is a very tedious task for real-time applications. Moreover, the challenge becomes more severe as new classes are added to the original database since predecessor class covariance matrices should be separately inserted into the equation (see Equations 2–4 and 2–5). In order to remedy these shortcomings, it was proposed that the transformation given by:

$$y = \begin{cases} \Delta_T \Delta_i^{-1} x, \text{ for training} \\ \Delta_T x, \text{ for post-training} \end{cases}$$
(2–5)

Where training phase $x \in C_i$, Δ_i and Δ_T are the covariance matrix of class C_i and overall dataset respectively.

The key element of this paradigm is the novel structure of the information processing system. The basic unit of an artificial neural network (ANN) is the neuron. Each neuron receives sums the weighted inputs, and passes the sum through a transfer function that can be a sigmoid. An ANN is an interconnected network of neurons. The input layer has one neuron for each of the each of the sensor signals, while the output layer has one neuron for each of the different sample properties that should be predicted. Generally, one hidden layer neuron with a variable number of neurons is places between the input and output layer. During the ANN training phase, the weights and transfer function parameters are updated such that the calculated output values for a set of input values are as close as possible to the known true values of the sample properties.

The odour recognition has to overcome problems caused by changes in odour due to food. These affect the constituents exuded from the sweat glands.

The use of artificial scents (deodorants/perfumes) will mask the natural body odours. To be effective the odour detector will need to search for base level of odours present at all times.

4.   MULTIMODAL BIOMETRICS

The multimodal biometric systems use multiple applications to capture different types of biometrics. This allows the integration of two or more types of biometric recognition systems. There could for example be a system combining fingerprint verification, facial recognition, voice recognition and other types of biometrics. The more biometric features that are measured, then it will be more difficult to attempt to fool the system. The amalgamation of a number of biometric recognition technologies, increases the chances of a positive identification being made, and compensates for the possibility of one of the biometrics providing a poor response. A number of factors should be considered when developing a multi-biometric system. These include the choice and number of biometric traits, the level in the biometric system at which the information provided by multiple traits should be integrated, the methodology used to integrate the information and the cost versus performance trade-off. (Jain, and Ross, 2004).

The choice of biometrics to be combined is determined by the nature of the application and the overheads, such as computational costs and the costs of the related hardware. In a mobile phone with a camera, it may be easier to combine facial recognition and voice recognition, but screens are now being developed which can double up as fingerprint scanners. In contrast an ATM application may find it easier to combine fingerprint and facial recognition. A commercial multi-biometric system called BioID is available which integrates the face, voice and the movement of the lips of an individual. The three biometric features are analysed simultaneously using a low cost implementation method, which only requires a standard USB camera and microphone. The system is easy to use and is unobtrusive; the user just looks into the camera and says their password. It has been applied in physical access control and in safeguarding ATM and financial transactions. For middleware to be successful standardised and the architectural issues have to be resolved. A key selling point for a number of companies is a single sign is insecure. The emergence of cost effective and mature biometric hardware has made this possible again.

It is more complicated, time consuming and expensive to develop a multimodal biometric system than it is to develop a single biometric system. Due to this complexity most multimodal databases developed so far only contain a few hundred individuals. This makes it more difficult to extrapolate the success or failure of a multimodal algorithm for use in a large-scale system covering millions of people. Current data protection legislation also prevents the exchange of such data across borders. The BIOSECURE European Network of Excellence has been tasked with evaluating the available multimodal biometric systems. It is evident that multimodal biometric systems require more research to determine whether they can be developed at a cost effective and efficient level. With most of the planned identity systems collecting multiple biometric information it is expected that in the future they will all be incorporated as a multimodal biometric system.

5.   BIOMETRIC ENCRYPTION

The biometric encryption is the process of using a characteristic of a person to code or scramble or un-scramble data. The individual physical characteristics (fingerprints, retinas and irises, palm prints, facial structure, and voice recognition) are encrypted. The reason that this new technology is believed to be superior to the use of passwords or personal identification numbers is that a biometric trait cannot be lost, stolen, and cannot be easily recreated, 'unless criminals are going to start cutting off peoples fingers to gain access to their accounts, but who knows what can happen'. The biometric encryption is based on mathematical process that helps to disguise the information contained in messages that is either transmitted or stored in a database, and there are three main factors that determine the security of any crypto system; the complexity of the mathematical process or algorithm, the length of the encryption key used to disguise the message, and safe storage of the key, known as key management. The length of the encryption key used to disguise the message is the next important piece of the encryption process. The shorter the encryption key length, the more vulnerable the data is to a "brute force" attack. This term refers to an individual trying to improperly access data by trying all combinations of possible passwords that would allow access to the account. In non-biometric encryption processes such as passwords or PIN numbers, depending on the length of the key, the information may be vulnerable to access by unauthorised users. For example, a key that is three characters long would be much more prone to attack than one that is ten characters long because the number of possible permutations that must be run to find the right key are much higher in the key that contains ten characters. With current computer power, it is estimated that it would take four hundred years to find the right access combination for a sixty-four-character key. Biometric encryption makes standard character encryption obsolete by replacing or supplementing the normal key characters with a personal identifier of the user that there can only be one perfect match for. Without this biometric key the information is inaccessible. The biometric encryption systems allow the user to transport the access key around without the need to make it vulnerable to be lost or stolen.

6. SUMMARY OF CHAPTER TWO

The major hurdle to implement biometrics globally at the consumer level is because of the wide diversity of competition, vendor-proprietary devices standardisation. The disharmony of biometric devices has promoted the protection of privacy, by restricting access of any one measurement to be used by other non-communicating systems, but in the long run it will create interoperability problems between vendors technology and global acceptance. Hence the compatibility of the system devices with necessary standards is necessary for global adaptation. A number of biometric devices are now available to capture biometric measurements, such as fingerprints, iris, retina, keystroke and voice. The accuracy of these systems does vary, which has a direct relevance on the levels of security, which they offer, and determines the areas in which they can be best utilised. The introduction of biometric measurement devices into any system will inevitably increase the levels of complexity of that system, which in itself can create problems. The next chapter exploits the applications of biometrics.

REFERENCES

Alonso-Fernandez, F., Fierrez-Aguilar, J., and Ortega-Garcia, J., 2005, *A Review of Schemes for Fingerprint Image Quality Computation: Biometrics Research Laboratory*, ATVS, Escuela Politecnica Superior: Universidad Autonoma de Madrid Avda, Spain.

B & J Biometrics, Inc., 2006, *Releases New Ultra Biometric Fingerprnt Encryption Mouse*, 2006, Press Release: http://www.biometrics-bj.com; http://news.thomasnet.com/ fullst ory/501662; and http://fingerprint.nist.gov/minex04 (February 20, 2007).

Baby R.E., Cabezas M., Walsoe de Reca E.N., 2000, 'Electronic nose: a useful tool for monitoring environmental contamination', *Sensors and Actuators*, Volume B 69, pp. 214–218.

Biometrics Consortium, 2005, *Introduction to Biometrics*, http://www.biome trics.htm (February 20, 2007).

Bourgeois, W., and Stuetz, R.M., 2000, 'Measuring wastewater quality using a sensor array: prospects for real-time monitoring', *Water SCI Techno*, Volume. 41 (12), pp. 107–112.

Brown, C. C., Zhang, X., Mersereau, R.M., and Clements M., 2002, 'Automatic Speech Reading with Application to Speaker Verification', *ICASSP International Conference on Acoustics, Speech and Signal Processing* (ICASSP).

Chirillo. S and Blaul. S, 2003, *Implementing Biometric Security*, John Wiley, Canada.

Davies, S.G., 1994, 'Touching the big brother: how biometric will fuse flesh and machine', *Information technology and people*, 7(4), http://biometrics.cse.msu.edu /publications. html#genbio (March 21, 2007).

Érdi, P., and Barna, G., 1991, 'Neurodynamic Approach to Odor Processing', *Proceeding of IEEE International Joint Conference on Neural Networks*, (IJCNN'91), Seattle, WA, USA.

Garcia-Salicetti, S., Beumier, S. Garcia-Salicetti, Beumier, C., Chollet, G., Dorizzi, B., Leroux-Les Jardins, J., Lunter, J., Ni, Y., Petrovska-Delacretaz, D., 2003, 'BIOMET: a Multimodal Person Authentication Database Including Face, Voice, Fingerprint, Hand and Signature Modalities', *Proceedings of 4th International Conference on Audio and Video-Based Biometric Person Authentication*, pp. 845–853, Guildford, UK.

Hong, L and Jain, A.K., 1998, 'Integrating faces and fingerprints for personal identification', *IEEE Transactions on PAMI*, vol. 20, http://biometrics.cse.msu.edu /publications. html#genbio (March 17, 2007).

Hong, L., 1998, *Automatic personal identification using fingerprints*, PhD Thesis: Michigan State University.

Huopio, S., 1998, *Biometric identification: Seminar on Network security, Authorization & Access control in open Network Environment*, www.tml.tkk.fi/Opinnot/Tik-110.501/1998/ papers/12biometric/biometric.htm (March 30, 2007).

Jain A, Griess F D, and Connell S D, 2002, *Online Signature Verification, Pattern Recognition*, vol. 35, No 12, December.

Jain, A., Hong, L., and Pankanti, S., 2000, 'Biometric Identification', *Communications of the ACM*: Vol. 43. No.2.

Jain, A.K., Bolle, R., and Pankanti, S., 1999, *Personal Identification in Networked society*, Kluwer Academic Publisher.

Jain, AK, Hong, L, Pankanti, S and Bolle, R., 1997, 'An identity authentication system using fingerprints', *Proceedings of the IEEE*, vol. 85, http://biometricscse .msu.edu/publicatio ns.html#genbio (March 7, 2007).

Lee, H.C. and Gaesslen, R.E., 2001, *Advances in Fingerprint Technology*, Elsevier, New York.

Li, Z., and Hopfield, J.J., 1989, 'Modeling the Olfactory Bulb and its Neural Oscillatory Processing', *Biological Cybernetics*, Volume 61, pp. 379–392.

Ly Van, B., Blouet, R., Renouard, S., Garcia-Salicetti, S., Dorizzi, B., Chollet, G., 2003, 'Signature with text-dependent and text-independent speech for robust identity verification', *Workshop on Multimodal User Authentication*, Santa Barbara, USA.

Maltoni, D., Maio, D., Jain, A., and Prabhakar, S., 2003, *Handbook of Fingerprint Recognition*, New York: Springer Verlag.

McLachlan, G.J., 1992, *Discriminant Analysis and statistical Pattern Recognition*, Wiley, New York.

Moenssens, A, A., 1971, *Fingerprint Techniques*, Chilton Book Co.

Nakamoto, T., et al., 1992, 'Gas/Odour Identification by Semiconductor Gas Sensor Array and an Analog Artificial Neural Network Circuit', *IEEE Proceeding of International Conference of Microelectronics (MIEL92)*, pp. 1–9.

Nakamoto, T., Nakahira, Y., Hiramatsu, H., 2001, 'Odor recorder using active odor sensing system', *Sensors and Actuators*, vol. B 76, pp. 465–469.

Nanvati, S., Thieme, M., 2002, *Biometrics- Identity Verification in a networked World*, John Wiley and Sons Inc.

Newham, E (1995) *Tthe biometric Report*. SJB Services, New York, http://sjb.co.uk (February 27, 2007).

Pankanti, S., Prabhakar, S., and Jain, A.K., 2002, 'Individuality of fingerprints', *IEEE Transactions on pattern analysis and machine intelligence*, vol.24, no.8, http://biometrics.cse.msu.edu/publications.html#genbio (March 27, 2007).

Prabhakar, S., and Jain, A.K., (2002), 'Decision-level fusion in fingerprint verification', *Pattern Recognition*, vol.35, no. 4.

Retica Systems, 2005, *Eye Technology-Retinal Biometric Technology*, Online at: http://www.retica.com/site/technology/index.html (February 19, 2007)

Ross, A., and Jain, A.K., 2003, 'Information fusion in biometrics', *Pattern Recognition Letters* 24, 13, September.

Ross, A., and Jain, A.K., 2004, 'Multibiometric Systems', *Communications of the ACM*, 2004, Vol. 47, No. 1.

Ross, A.A., 2003, *Information fusion in fingerprint authentication*, PhD Thesis: Michigan State University.

Sandström, M. *Liveness detection in fingerprint recognition systems*, Linköpig University Electronic Press, Thesis, June 2004, http://www.ep.liu.se (March 22, 2007).

Technews, 2005, 'Biometric systems based on capacitance sensing technology', *Security Solutions*, http://securitysa.com/article.asp?pklArticleid=1774&pklIssueID=248&pklCaeryID=21 (January 31, 2007).

Temel,T., and Karlik B., 2007, 'An Improved Odor Recognition System Using Learning Vector Quantization with a New Discriminant Analysis', *Proceeding of the International Conference on Digital communication and Computer Applications, (DCCA 2007)*, Jordan.

Womack, M. 1994, 'The Eyes Have It', *Sensor Review*, Volume 14, No 4.

Woodward D. John, Orlans M. Nicholas, Higgins T. Peter, 2003, *Biometrics: Identity Assurance in the Information Age*, Mc Graw Hill.

Chapter 3

APPLICATIONS OF BIOMETRICS

1. INTRODUCTION

Many of the inherent limitations, which are peculiar to biometrics technologies, are discussed in previous chapters. Any organisation considering introducing biometrics systems must determine their requirements and choose the system which best meets their needs. Throughout the development process consultations should be made between developers, managers and the users to detect any problems and concerns, which should be resolved immediately before implementation. Any biometric system installed must be ethically sound.

"Knowledge is the beginning of practice; doing is the completion of knowing."

—Wang Yang-Ming (1498)

The concerns over any dangers in using biometrics must be taken seriously and the users should be confident that when they use a biometrics system it is safe and their data is secure and held in confidence. Legal measures may need to be introduced to regulate and protect users' privacy. This chapter is based on cost effectiveness and the applications of biometrics.

2. ECONOMY OF SCALE

The cost of biometric sensors has continued to reduce due to advances in technology, improved manufacturing efficiency and the economy of scale. In the future sensors will become more compact with new applications. The Bank Hapoalim in Israel and the Nationwide Building Society in the UK have introduced dynamic signature verification systems. Numerous airports around the world are installing or trailing systems at the port of entry. In healthcare the move towards electronic records has increased the demand for biometric security features. There has been much initiative from governments worldwide to integrate biometrics into the driving licenses, identity cards and passports with a move towards silicon sensors, which are more robust. The iris recognition has also continued to increase in popularity especially in the immigration and travel sectors.

For the biometrics technologies to work effectively on a global basis there are needs for standards. Since 2006 the UK Home Office have started issuing the biometric passports to replace the non-biometrics. It is also hope that there will be identity card information added. The applicant will need to attend a local enrolment centre (over 70% being set up in the UK), where the photograph, signature, iris and fingerprint will be scanned. After the enrolment the applicant receives a card, which incorporates the biometric scans and a photograph alongside other personal information, which can be used to confirm the identity of that person. For verification purposes there is a need for standards to be established. No country will want to have to install multiple readers for passports. Verification can either be with information held on the card or there can be a link with the central database.

3.   SECURITY ACCESS

Biometrics systems are particularly useful in controlling physical access to secure buildings or rooms. A number of biometrics has been applied; either as single system or a multimodal system (a number of biometric or other identity measures are combined to increase security). Passwords and identity cards can be stolen, lost or forgotten, but a biometric measure is always present on the body of the authorised user.

At Disney world in Orlando, Florida, biometric hand recognition technology is used to ensure that one person uses only one mulple-day ticket. The park tickets are valid for a number of days, so linking the validity of the ticket to a handprint prevents the tickets being passed on to a third party.

In schools, biometrics are used to track children and to keep a check on enrolment and attendance. It could quickly be established if a child had not turned up for class, or had left part way through the day without permission. In the USA many children are transported to school by bus, there is sometimes a problem with children getting the wrong bus; biometrics could be used for access to the bus, with the child only allowed access to the correct bus.

Efforts have also been made to make air travel easier for frequent flyers, as part of a US government goal to reduce airport check in times to less than 10 minutes. The airlines can introduce a two tier check-in system. The frequent flyers would apply for a smart card, at a charge, undergo background checks and provide palm geometry and facial recognition data. This data could then be checked against a central database. Many airlines though do not want to commit to the expense of implementing smart cards, since no industry standards have yet been set. Smart cards have also been introduced to the US Defence department to allow staff to have access to military bases and secure networks (Boyd, 2001).

Many major retailers are showing an interest in using biometrics because of fraudulent transactions and identity theft, biometrics has proven to be successful in combating these types of fraud. The technology at the moment has not been widely applied, it is only present in small chains that use the technology for secure cashing of cheques, or it is being used on a trial basis only.

The introduction of chip and pin credit and debit cards has reduced card fraud but it is not a fully secure system, since PIN's can be found out and cards can still be fraudulently produced. To increase security during online transactions MasterCard has introduced 'MasterCard SecureCode' and Visa has introduced 'Verified by VISA', which allows customers to set up passwords for use with online transactions. Criminal groups always try to keep ahead of changes and any security measure will be faced with unauthorised people trying to get access. Recent research has shown that implementing biometrics measures is likely to deter fraudsters. The dominant biometric feature is the use of fingerprints, due to its low cost, high levels of accuracy and its ease of use. Voice recognition has been used in telephone transactions to identify the caller, and keystroke dynamics, facial recognition and signature verification are also used in many other ways but there accuracy is very questionable.

The BioPay company has developed a system to record customers' fingerprints to authorise their personal cheques when used in shops. To use the system for the first time a fingerprint template and other information is taken from the customers. This template is stored in a central BioPay database, which is then used to verify the identity of the individual. If a cheque is returned, it is flagged against that person in the system. This information is then shared with all of the other stores linked up to the BioPay database. The cheque authentication system could quite easily be extended to the use of credit and debit cards. Some systems are currently being trailed which allow fingerprints to be used instead of a PIN when making card transactions. The fingerprints are held on a central database, and are then combined with the information recorded by the point of sale terminal and then authorises the transaction if it meets the necessary criteria. To become widespread, the system needs to convince the privacy community about its levels of security.

A system developed by U-Check has been installed at a chain of convenience stores in Utah, which uses the customers' fingerprints to recognise them. The customers are able to put their own shopping through a check out and pay the bill. To exit the store and prevent theft, they have to confirm their identity, which is then linked in to a record of their transaction; if both match then the exit gate opens. The Discover card in the US has entered into a partnership with Pay By Touch to allow customers to include reward cards, credit cards, and bank information, which is used to build a personal Pay By Touch wallet, stored at secure IBM data centres. Access to the stored accounts is then by fingerprint recognition (Ingram, 1999; Powell, 2004). The initial thrust for the development of biometrics in retail sector is likely to come from online transactions. To use biometrics for online shopping, each shopper must be able to submit a biometric sample. To do this fingerprint scanners will need to become widely available, cheap and preferably incorporated into the keyboard or into the mouse. There are many challenges involved to get this system to work. The biometrics system can be use to monitor the time keeping and absenteeism of members of staff. It is also capable of monitoring who has access to cash registers at particular times. The systems can help to reduce thefts and access restriction and it could have a part to play in increasing security at ATM, but so far the emergence of biometrics in this area has been slow.

4.   POLICE AND PRISON SERVICES

The police and prison services have access to large amounts of sensitive personal information. Biometrics would be an ideal method to make sure that officers can only access information they are authorised to access. The police have their own mobile Closed Circuit TeleVision (CCTV) units. With the advent of computers, vast databases have been created which allow an identification to be made within seconds. Fingerprints and other biometrics can be used to access files for investigation and to enter restricted areas. Fixed and mobile CCTV systems can be used to monitor members of the public, which, when combined with facial recognition software allows the police to identify people from within a crowd. The mobile CCTV is often used to monitor crowds at football matches and other gatherings, for troublemakers. The facial biometrics can also be applied to any CCTV footage seized during an investigation where the image can be taken and matched with a police database. On the other hand, voice recognition software are used for identify the voice patterns under investigation, which can also be matched with data already held, or data that can be collected at a later date.

The large prisons in UK have installed a hand geometry recognition system to identify the visitors. To meet the requirements of the Learmont and Woodcock reports, visitors have to be identified by two different methods when entering and leaving the prison. This is to ensure that a prisoner does not walk out of the prison in place of the visitor. The chosen method is hand geometry linked to a photograph of the visitor. New visitors have their photograph taken, and their hand geometry is measured and stored. At subsequent visits the processing of the visitor is reduced since the relevant data is already held on the database. The database also allows a record to be kept of who visits the prisoner, and when. The prison doctors at the South-West Dorset Primary Care Trust (SWDPCT) in the UK are being asked to use fingerprint recognition technology to access patient records and sign off medication. The doctors are issued with a user ID and also using a fingerprint keyboard reader to verify their identity before retrieving and updating an inmates health records. All records are linked to a centralised database, enabling them to be accessed by external practitioners if required. The data is not copied or distributed, and the prisoners can decide if they want external doctors to be allowed to view parts of their data. The biometric system also extends to prisoners receiving medication.

5.   PATIENT MANAGEMENT IN HOSPITALS

Most patient records are now held electronically, it is important that anyone who uses the system can only access information that is relevant to the jobs they are doing. The electronic records are available not just in hospital but also in the community through the General Practitioner (GP) service. There is also the necessity to make sure that the correct patient details are being accessed, for example a ward may have two patients with the same name. While the health care sector has incorporated electronic medical records, data repositories, networking and Internet access into its various processes, the corresponding security measures have not been enhanced. In the US measures have been put in place, which only allows patients medical records to be accessed by individuals directly involved with their treatment and health care operations. Other health care users need the patients' permission to access information. There is also the requirement that only the minimum necessary level of information is released to the user. Within many hospitals, wireless networks are now being installed that allow the use of tablet PC's to retrieve patient information. The provision of wireless networks is now becoming common in hospitals, which also raises new concerns about security of records held on the system; measures will have to be taken to prevent eavesdroppers from accessing the system (Krawczyk and Jain, 2005).

Potentially biometrics could be used to keep track of patients, and prevent them from having the wrong procedures carried out or mistakenly be given the wrong drugs. The patient could have their fingerprints taken on admission; the prints would then be checked whenever treatments are administered. This would be especially useful for seriously ill, elderly or mentally ill patients who may have difficulty communicating. Elderly people in the community with conditions such as 'Alzheimer's', who may wander off, then get confused and lost, could then have their fingerprints and photographs lodged with the police, so they can be identified and returned safely. The biometric authorisation is seen as offering a number of advantages over the traditional identity card and password systems. A number of systems have been developed, which incorporate fingerprint recognition and iris recognition into the authorisation process. So far they have not been widely applied, but in the future it is likely to be used for access to computers, patient information and to identify patients and staff for treatment and access to different parts of the hospital. With free healthcare available in some countries, like UK, there are a significant number of patients who present themselves, but they do not have the correct paperwork. To receive treatment, or to register with a GP, the a person will need to provide proof of identity and address. Emergency treatment would still be provided, but this would stop people coming into the country to receive treatment for non-life threatening conditions.

In the Canadian province of Ontario there is concern that the health system has nearly 12 million patients enrolled, but the province only has a population of 10 million. It is perceived that many US citizens are using the system without entitlement. The system is likely to involve digitised photographs and hand geometry stored on a central database. Each user would be issued with a plastic identity card, with a magnetic strip, containing a facial image, date of birth, security features and a fingerprint. Authorised users at multiple sites can use data scanned from a person's hand to search the database for matches. The system will also need to interface with existing computer networks. The savings made in administrative and payments systems would recoup the cost of installing and maintaining the system (Davies, 1994).

Benefit agencies distributing pensions, unemployment and sickness benefits in a number of countries have introduced biometric technology to prevent fraudulent or duplicate claims. The Spanish system stores a fingerprint scan on a smart card which is used to provide verification, similar systems have been introduced in South Africa, the Philippines and some states in the US.

6. CASINO FACIAL RECOGNITION

The gaming industry has shown interest in establishing and ensuring identities by using of biometrics. In casino cash rooms and operation centres where millions of dollars are potentially at stake, only individuals whose identities have been examined and verified can be admitted. Casinos have been at the forefront of developments in facial recognition technology. It is possible for a group of people to be able to manipulate the games in their favour using card counting. To prevent excessive losses the casinos use facial biometric information. This information is shared with other casinos. Should the person try to enter the casino, the CCTV cameras can be monitored and images used to provide a match with the database of people the casino does not wish to allow entry.

The hundreds of cameras on the floor of the casino, searched for anyone who matched the held data. The data was run through the Griffin database of suspected card counters, to make identification. The teams of card counters left Las Vegas for Europe but the technology followed them, with the European casinos being in contact with the US casinos (Horizon, 2004). The facial recognition is now widely employed by casinos. This has also led to a global database of players that the casinos do not wish to enter their establishments. The international network is known as the Surveillance Information Network (SIN), which links over 140 casino surveillance rooms, to protect their interests. Three of Atlantic City's twelve casinos use a facial recognition system developed by M.I.T. which recognises specific facial features, in the national database, which is then transmitted to other databases around the world, anyone who pays for the service can have access to it. Some casinos in London have signed up for a system, which allows live footage of players to be transmitted from their casino to the headquarters of the Anderson program in Las Vegas for identity investigation. The legality of this is questionable and is under investigation. A legal ruling has already been made in Ontario, Canada, that without the knowledge of the customers the casinos cannot use facial recognition systems. A number of casinos also use hand readers to allow authorised staff to enter restricted areas.

7.   ENTERPRISE NETWORK SECURITY AND WEB ACCESS

Many companies have internal networks where security of information has to be maintained, with only authorised users able to access it. With the growth of the Internet, there is now a need to restrict access to sensitive data on the web to authorised users only. The web services depend upon the Internet Protocol (IP) name service. If an impostor gains access to the name service, the security based upon correlating names and the network address will fail. The traditional method of authentication involves using usernames and passwords, which are openly transmitted across the network. Passwords can be made more secure by using encryption but not 100 per cent secured. The biometric authentication eliminates the need to remember passwords. The person also needs to be physically present at the time of authentication. At present, biometric sensors need to be reduced in price and their efficiency needs to be improved, if they are to be incorporated into other technologies. Some usable features such as digital cameras and microphones are already low cost additions to computer systems.

Jain *et al.*, 1998 developed an authentication method based on hand geometry. Each biometric measure has its own strengths and limitations, which make them suitable for particular authentication applications. In high security applications, fingerprints are preferred, but in a network situation too much information could be revealed about a person's fingerprint, which could compromise the identity of the individual. Hand geometry was chosen since it is specific enough for verification, but not very accurate for identification. People also seem to be more comfortable with hand geometry, rather than fingerprints. The system involves the user positioning his hand on a template, an image is then taken and measurements are made. In enrolment five measurements are taken, and 16 features such as finger length are extracted from the image. In verification the image has to match one of the stored images.

It is important that biometric data is encrypted before it is passed over the public network. This reduces the risk of the data being intercepted and misused. It is also critical that all templates in a distributed biometrics system are securely stored. This prevents the biometric template of an authorised user being extracted for other purposes, or an attacker could substitute his template in place of that of the legitimate user. The policies concerning access management must also be stored securely; these policies should be enforced in a secure manner. It is important that simplicity in using the network or web systems should not be compromised by introducing biometric verification. To function fully, a flexible, ubiquitous, platform-independent computing environment is needed for distributed biometric systems (Rragami and Edwards, 2003).

Emerging XML-based standards such as WS-Security, XCBF and SAML are helping to bring biometrics and web services together. These provide improved and agreed ways to send data in web service requests. At its destination it decrypted and compared with security data and access is then either granted or denied. To become widely available the cost barriers will need to be overcome as well as setting international standards that all PC manufacturers can incorporate the relevant technology. Many companies are also wary about being tied into the software and hardware from one particular company, since this limits their flexibility for future updates.

Biometrics could provide increased security against online crime, but it will need major investment by the banks to provide all the users with the relevant equipment. There will be a trade off; it will only be introduced if the costs of implementation and maintenance are less than what is being lost to fraud. The ING bank in Canada uses a computer mouse with an embedded fingerprint scanner to improve security of online transactions. The reducing cost of biometric equipment will increases the inevitability that biometrics will become commonplace in everyday life. It may though be too costly to add biometric features to an existing computer network; it will be much more cost effective to have biometrics incorporated into any future upgrades to the network (Shoniregun 2005).

8.   CONCEPTUAL CLIENT REQUIREMENTS

Many challenges are encountered when developing biometric system. The conceptual client requirements can be either a stand-alone biometrics, with no internal or external links, which may also be incorporated into an existing system. The initial stage should be a discussion between the designer and the user to ascertain what the exact requirements of the system are to be. The user needs to balance out the increased costs of using biometrics, against the increased level of security, which is offered. From our research findings the main reason given by the organisations that participated in questionnaire survey was that the integrating biometrics to the existing security system would increase the level of security to near 100 per cent. It must be remembered that any system must have a backup, should the main system fail. It is also necessary to provide a shortlist of biometrics systems to the user, to see systems in operation. However, factors to be examined when choosing biometrics systems are the operational costs, the cost and time needed to enrol each user, and the sensitivity of the system. The sensitivity can be set by the user and will vary depending on whether the level of security is high or low. The most underestimated cost is the enrolment. Part of the outcome of the questionnaire survey shows that individual's first encounter with the biometric system often requires assistance, the costs of this can be kept down by streamlining the enrolment procedure to maximise the chances of high quality enrolments, and the production of stable templates. If the templates collected are robust then this will lead to lower support costs during operation (Rejman-Greene, 2003).

Furthermore, a Privacy Impact Assessment (PIA) should be carried out to examine the legal issues surrounding the deployment. The PIA would be used has a consultation platform for users to elicit concerns about using the system, before the system is installed. As we mention above, the type of backup system should also be examined since it can be very costly to implement. If the system is well designed then the number of users needing to resort to the backup system should be minimal. Much of the success of biometrics depends upon the cooperation of the user, so it is not a good idea to alienate them, they should be brought on board at an early stage in the development process. There are also established standards and to a limited extent for the interchange of files of biometric data. Other standards are also still under development. Once the most cost effective and robust biometrics to be implemented has been agreed, it should be trailed in real life situations to discover any problems with the software, the hardware or the ease of use by the user. Any problems can be rectified at this stage and the system can be rolled out.

8.1 Enhancement of passport and identity card systems

There is a need for biometric passport and identity cards, due to the increased security threats perceived by governments around the world. To implement the introduction of these measures changes will have to be made to the way in which these documents are processed and used. The user will need to apply for the passport and identity cards by filling out a form and providing proof of their identity. The cards could also incorporate driving licences, and information about the users NHS and national insurance numbers. Other information such as medical conditions and emergency contact details could also be included. The initial stage of processing will require the user to attend a centre to have their fingerprints and retinal/iris scans taken. Our recommendation would be for this to be carried out at the local police station or local government offices within a country, since people should not be inconvenienced by having to travel long distances to a processing centre.

The user's data and the biometrics measurements would be held in a central database and in the chip embedded in the card. When the card is used the user will provide a biometric measurement, which can then be compared with data held on the chip or the central database. For this to function effectively there will need to be international standards laid down, or as is likely a number of standards come into use, they will all need to be compatible. If the biometric data is not a satisfactory match with the data held on the passport then it should be possible to get extra information from a central database. Data would be recorded on when you enter or leave a country, which can then also be automatically transferred to your home country system. The identity cards would be needed to access benefits and health services, as well as anywhere that may require identity checks such as opening a bank account. Under this system we envisage that the passport being replaced with a passport card, incorporating an identity card, driving licence, national insurance information, NHS number and vital health information e.g. allergies, chronic conditions and medication. It should also be flexible and able to be regularly updated. There is an ethical problem with having a card that holds so much information, so measures have to be put in place to allow authorised access only to appropriate information, e.g. health staff should only be able to read the medical information, and the police should only have access to address and driving licence information. The Figures 3–1 to 3–10 presents instances of how to secured biometric applications using use cases and activity diagrams for in-depth illustration.

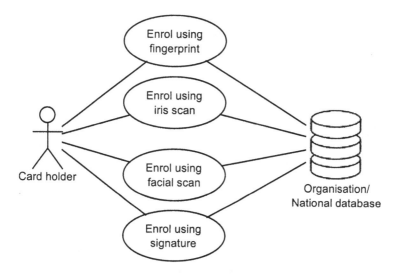

Figure 3–1. Enrolment procedure, for passports and identity cards

The card holder provides the relevant biometric information, which is in-corporated into the database, by the database administrator (see Figure 3–1 for diagrammatic illustration).

The relevant biometric information provided by the applicant/card holder is compared with the data held in the database, under the control of the data-base administrator (see Figure 3–2 for diagrammatic illustration and chapter 4 for further discussion).

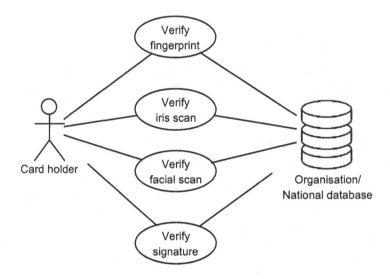

Figure 3–2. Verification procedure for passports and identity cards

Whenever the cardholder is required to provide biometric information, it is compared with the template stored in the database. The identity of the cardholder is then confirmed or denied. The official card reader encompasses all the bodies that may request biometric information, such as immigration, police, benefits agency and the health service (see Figures 3–3 and 3–4 for diagrammatic illustration and chapter 4 for further discussion).

For enrolment, the fingerprint, iris and signature need to be taken more than once, they are then combined to produce the template. The template is held in the national database to be used for comparisons during the verifica-tion process. The information held on the database is also held on the smart card chip so that identification can be made (see Figure 3–5 for diagrammatic illustration and chapter 4 for further discussion).

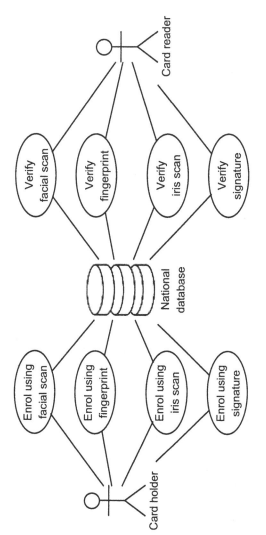

Figure 3–3. Card reader

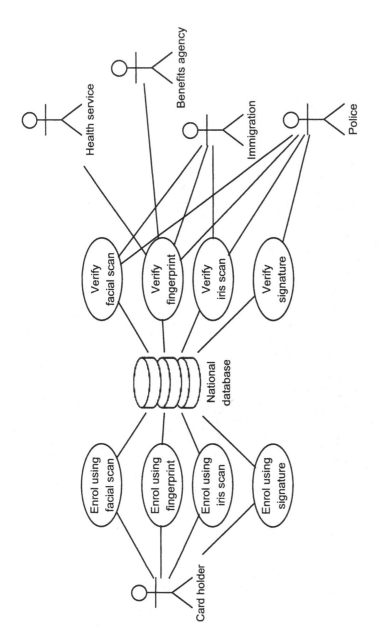

Figure 3–4. Verification link

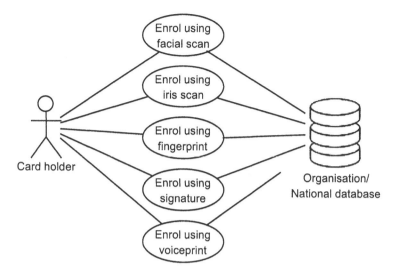

Figure 3–5. Detailed enrolment procedure

At immigration control, when the passport is checked, a photograph of the passport holder is taken, a fingerprint is recorded and an iris scan may be used as a back-up for instance if the fingerprint scan was unsuccessful (see Figure 3-6 for diagrammatic illustration).

If a person is suspected of drink driving and stopped by the police, they will have their identity checked by way of a portable fingerprint reader linked via mobile technology to a national database, or by using fixed biometric devices at a police station. If the person's identity cannot be confirmed at this stage then further identity checks will need to be made, not necessarily of a biometric variety (see Figure 3–7 for diagrammatic illustration).

The police station has a direct link to the national database that replicate data to the local databases, which can be used to update or identify people who are brought into the station. The identity checks here will be fingerprint, iris and facial recognition. Once identity has been confirmed it can link to police database to detect any previous offences. If identity cannot be confirmed then it is up to the person under investigation to provide evidence of their true identity, as mentioned above the data will be input to update the main database (see Figure 3–8 for diagrammatic illustration).

To prevent multiple claims under multiple identities, the 'Benefits Agency' will use the identity card and a fingerprint scans to confirm the identity of the claimant. Using one biometric will make the system simpler to operate, but

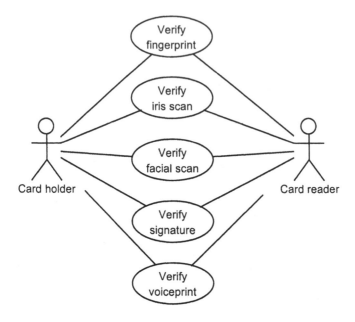

Figure 3–6. Immigration identification procedure

we highly recommended multimodal biometrics approach (see Figure 3–9 for diagrammatic illustration).

Foreign nationals who are claming free health care that they are not entitled to, would be required to provide an identity card and a fingerprint, which can be used to confirm their identity. For a patient found unconscious, with no identity cards, their fingerprints could be used to give a preliminary identification and it would allow the medical staff to access medical records to help in assessing the patient needs(see Figure 3–10 for diagrammatic illustration).

The enrolment procedure requires the user to register their biometrics data. The templates produced are stored in the national biometric database, together with all the other personal information that has been collected. The applicant receives an identity card and/or passport, which also contains the biometric data. The card holder needs to be verified and provides the biometrics requested, which are used to identify him/her against certain criteria.

In actual operation the complexity of the verification and identification procedure will depend on the requirements of the body requesting the biometric information. The highest security levels will be in immigration and the police, where they need to be absolutely certain of a person's identity. The health service and the benefits agency will operate at a lower level since they just wish to

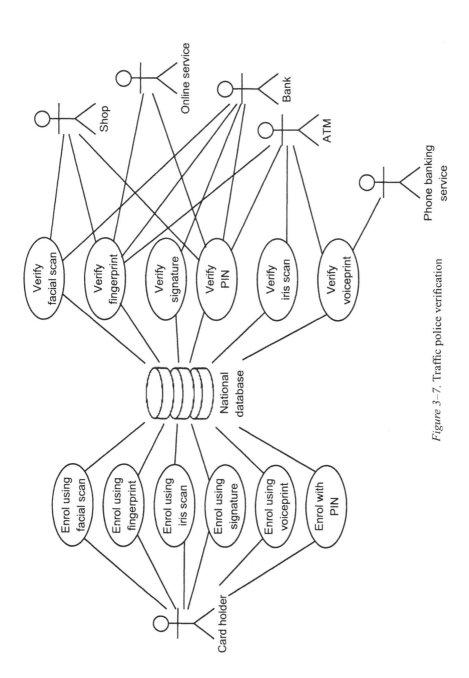

Figure 3–7. Traffic police verification

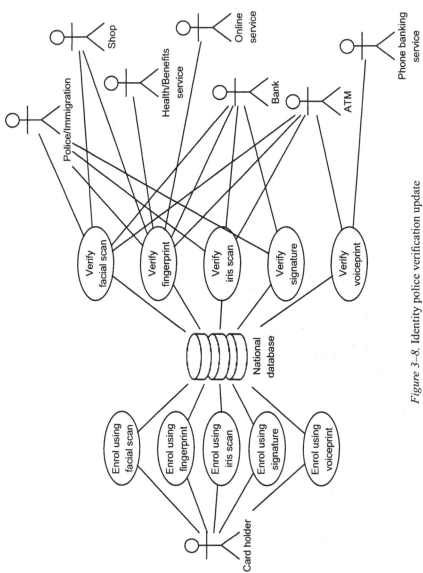

Figure 3–8. Identity police verification update

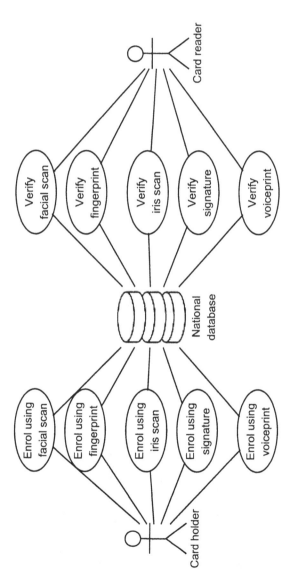

Figure 3–9. Benefits agency identification procedure

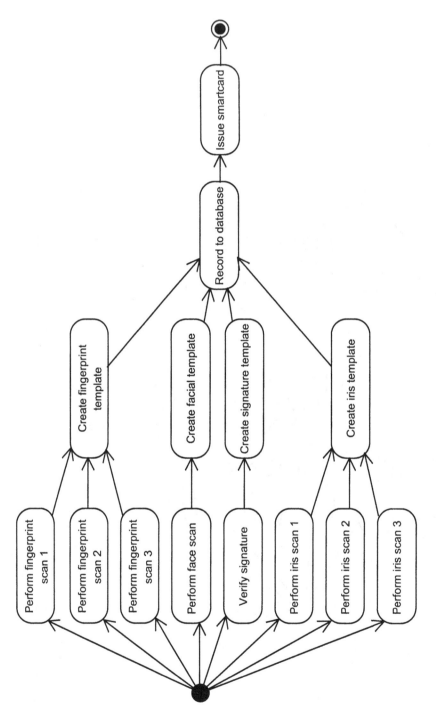

Figure 3–10. Health service identification

verify a person's identity and address. The police and immigration utilise multiple biometrics, but the health service and the benefits agency will only use fingerprints for identification, but we recommend multi-modal biometrics.

The immigration will initially use fingerprint and facial scans, if the identification is rejected or is ambiguous, the iris scan is taken as a backup. The traffic police will use portable fingerprint readers, while at police stations extra methods will be available. In all cases if the biometric measure fails then there is a provision for a repeat sample to be taken. The UK identity biometric cards are required to reduce the incidence of identity theft, control illegal immigration and working, control access to public services and to enhance general security. The scheme will be delivered by a new agency, incorporating the UK Passport Service, with the Immigration and Nationality Directorate of the Home Office. The proposed UK Home Office identity card system has four main components:

i.   An enrolment service when there will be a personal interview to deal with the application and to obtain the facial image, iris and fingerprint biometrics. The enrolment centres will be local, probably in police stations or council offices, with the provision of a mobile service for remote areas.

ii. The National Identity Register will be a new, highly secure database holding personal information. Information will not be placed on the system until it has been checked by the enrolment service.

iii. The ID cards will be issued as either stand-alone documents or alongside other documents such as passport or drivers licence. The residence permits issued to foreign nationals would also act as ID cards.

iv. A verification service that provides a secure, convenient way to prove identity: when opening a bank account, or registering with a GP. It links the person's ID cards with their record on the register, but it will fail if matching information cannot be found. The verification service will work on different levels to suit the needs of the user. For example, it may just confirm a card is valid or it may provide some restricted information.

The number of times a biometric measure can be repeated will be decided by the system rules that have been agreed upon and the alternative biometrics profile requests at different time. The proposed identity security card is based on the following measures:

i.   People will need to apply in person, so that personal identification such as date of birth, name and address can be checked with other identification to see if they match. This will prevent cases of impersonation.

ii. Unique biometric information such as fingerprints and iris patterns will be recorded when the person applies. This information should be recorded in just a few minutes, and will allow the system to detect people who try to establish more than one identity.

iii. At present the identification of forged identity documents relies on the skill of the person checking the document. The new identity cards will be checked electronically with data held on the National Identity Register. This will provide a highly secure and reliable means for public and private sector organisations to check identity.

A trial of the proposed biometric passport was carried out using a booth equipped with biometric enrolment devices. The devices were a camera, an electronic signature pad, a fingerprint scanner and an iris scanner. The person being recorded was not directly supervised, but staff were available should difficulties be encountered. The process involved a photograph, and the biometric scans; the card was then produced and tested for verification purposes. The enrolment time was an average of 7 minutes 56 seconds, which includes a one to many database checks, to see if they were already registered, which averaged at 90 seconds. Verification times were also checked, facial verification took 39 seconds, iris verification took 58 seconds and fingerprint verification took 1minute 13 seconds. The times for those with disabilities were slightly longer. All the biometrics apart from facial recognition produced a good match, but facial recognition only had a 69% success rate (Atos Origin 2005). The verification phases will determines whether a person is who they claim to be. It can be done with either centralised storage or with distributed storage. It is a 1 to 1 matching, where the live data is compared with the expected stored data for that person. A centralised database is compiled at enrolment, which is then used to compare the data collected at the time of examination. The alternative is for the biometric data to be stored in a memory device that can be carried by the individual. The live sample is compared with the biometric data held on the memory device. Both methods are susceptible to false acceptance and false rejects but the memory device is more susceptible to tampering and forgery. The UK Identity Card Bill requires 49 separate pieces of information to be stored on the identity card, which are detailed below:

i.   Personal information

- Full name.

- Other names by which person is or has been known.

- Date of birth.

- Place of birth.

- Gender.

- Address of principal place of residence in the United Kingdom.

- The address of every other place in the United Kingdom where person has a place of residence.

ii. Identifying information

- A photograph of head and shoulders.

- Signature.

- Fingerprints.

- Other biometric information.

iii. Residential status

- Nationality.

- Entitlement to remain in the United Kingdom where that entitlement derives from a grant of leave to enter or remain in the United Kingdom, the terms and conditions of that leave.

iv. Personal reference numbers

- National Identity Registration Number.

- The number of any ID card issued.

- Allocated national insurance number.

- The number of any relevant immigration document.

- The United Kingdom passport number.

- The number of any passport issued to the individual by or on behalf of the authorities of a country or territory outside the United Kingdom or by or on behalf of an international organisation.

- The number of any document that can be used by them (in some or all circumstances) instead of a passport.

- The number of any identity card issued to him/her by the authorities of a country or territory outside the United Kingdom.

- Any reference number allocated to him/her by the secretary of state in connection with an application made by him for permission to enter or to remain in the United Kingdom.

- The numbers of any work permit relating to him/her.

- Any driver number given to him/her by a driving licence.

- The number of any designated document which is held by him/her and is a document the number of which does not fall within any of the preceding sub-paragraphs.

- The date of expiry or period of validity of a document the number of which is recorded by virtue of this paragraph.

v. Record history

- Information falling within the preceding paragraphs that has previously been recorded about him/her in the Register.

- Particulars of changes affecting that information and of changes made to his/her entry in the Register.

- Date of death.

vi. Registration and ID card history

- The date of every application for registration made by him/her.

- The date of every application by him/her for a modification of the contents of his entry.

- The date of every application by him/her confirming the contents of his entry (with or without changes).

- The reason for any omission from the information recorded in his/her entry.

- Particulars (in addition to its number) of every ID card issued to him/her.

- Whether each such card is in force and, if not, why not.

- Particulars of every person who has countersigned an application by him/her for an ID card or a designated document, so far as those particulars were included on the application.

- Particulars of every notification given about lost, stolen and damaged ID cards

- Particulars of every requirement by the secretary of state for the individual to surrender an ID card issued to him.

vii. Validation information

- The information provided in connection with every application to be entered in the Register, for a modification of the contents of his entry or for the issue of an ID card.

- The information provided in connection with every application confirming entry in the Register (with or without changes).

- Particulars of the steps taken, in connection with an application mentioned above or otherwise, for identifying the applicant or for verifying the information provided in connection with the application.

- Particulars of any other steps taken or information obtained for ensuring that there is a complete, up-to-date and accurate entry about that individual in the Register.

- Particulars of every notification given by that individual for changing details in the register.

viii.   Security information

- A personal identification number to be used for facilitating the making of applications for information recorded in his/her entry, and for facilitating the provision of the information.

- A password or other code to be used for that purpose or particulars of a method of generating such a password or code.

- Questions and answers to be used for identifying a person seeking to make such an application or to apply for or to make a modification of that entry.

ix. Records of provision of information

- Particulars of every occasion on which information contained in the individual's entry have been provided to a person.

- Particulars of every person to whom such information has been provided on such an occasion.

- Other particulars in relation to each such occasion, of the provision of the information.

Apart from the UK, there are growing numbers of countries producing, requiring or preparing to introduce machine-readable travel documents. For this to work biometric standards need to be introduced. The ICAO TAG MRTD/ NTWG (2004) proposes the following guideline:

i.   Global Interoperability. The specifications for the use of biometrics must have a universally interoperable condition.

ii. Uniformity. Using standards to minimise the different solutions may be adopted by different states.

iii. Technical Reliability. The provision of guidelines and parameters to ensure member states deploy highly reliable technologies, and that data read is of a high enough quality.

iv. Practicality. The need to ensure that recommended standards could be made operational and implemented without the need to have a large number of disparate systems and equipment.

v. Durability. The systems introduced should last at least 10 years, and future updates should be backward compatible.

Furthermore, the application of biometric technologies on a global basis should include the following:

i. Specification of a primary interoperable form of biometric technology for use at border control, e.g. verification and watch lists, as well as by carriers and document issuers and specifications of agreed supplementary biometric technologies.

ii. Specification of the biometric technologies to be used by document issuers.

iii. Capability of retrieving information for maximum (10 years) validity for travelling document.

iv. To have no proprietary element to ensure that any states investing in biometrics are protected against changing infrastructure or changing suppliers.

For global interoperability biometrics software has to be written in such a way that other biometrics devices can easily interpret it.

8.2   Secure banking and other transactions

There has been an increasing problem with the use of ATM's, the cards could easily be 'skimmed' or copied. To increase security in banking transactions, multimodal biometrics approach should be adopted. When the customer applies for a card the usual checks are carried out. Before the card is issued the customer will now be required to attend a local branch to give fingerprint and facial recognition data. At this time they will also need to provide confirmation of identity and address. The information collected is then held on a central database. The card contained customer's data but not the biometric information, since this is held centrally, the embedded chip in the card stored confirmation data that would allow the card to be use in shops, should the network fail. In the initial stages the card will need to operate as a chip and pin card while the new equipment is rolled out into shops and ATM's. To maintain simplicity and ease of use the equipment in shops will read just fingerprints, but ATM's will be able to read fingerprints, iris scans and facial features.

The use of the card in shops will involve the customer placing a finger on a reader; measurements will be taken, which are then compared with information on the card and the central database. At the time of confirmation a digital photograph could be generated on the point of sale terminal to allow the cashier to visually confirm the identity of the cardholder, before completing the transaction. Confirmation would be received in the same way as chip and pin, before the transaction is confirmed. The ATM's will carry out a similar process but with the added security of facial recognition. Transactions in bank branches can also take advantage of the use of facial recognition, fingerprints and signature verification, to enhance the levels of security.

Credit and debit card transactions carried out online also need to be made more secure. It is not secure to provide the card number and the three digits on the back of the card. Keyboards are already being produced with fingerprint readers, which are used to access the network instead of a password and can also be adopted to make online transactions more secure (see chapter 4 further discussion). The process would be similar to that used in shops. With the introduction of national identity cards containing biometric information, it may be feasible to link together the biometrics data taken for the identity card with the banks systems. This would reduce costs, since the banks will not have to carry out biometric enrolment.

According to Visa UK there were 4.6 billion card transactions during the second quarter of 2005, so the database will need to be effectively run, and provide a confirmation of the transaction within seconds. This will require considerable processing power. The most complex biometrics will be at ATM's, where the methods can be automated and allows considerable opportunities for back up, should one of the systems fail. We do not expect the ATM to measure all of the biometrics every time a card is used, it will usually authorise using just one of the measures. Online transactions will utilise just fingerprint scanners, which can easily be incorporated into computer keyboards or a mouse. This could also be combined with the newly introduced online password schemes such as 'Verified by Visa', to provide added security. Telephone banking would make use of voice recognition to ensure that the caller is the genuine cardholder. The credit card fraud take place at ATM's, where cards can be skimmed, or 'card –trapping (Card appears jammed in machine, but criminal knows how to release it) can take place. Significant amount of fraud occurs abroad, the forged cards being taken overseas, or travellers having cards stolen. The major area of fraud is now in Internet transactions, especially since the introduction of chip and PIN technology has made it more difficult to carry out illegal face-to-face transactions. To combat CNP fraud, a number of strategies have been proposed (Cardwatch, 2005):

i. *Address Verification System* (AVS) and *Card Security Code* (CSC), allow online businesses to verify the customers billing address and a special security code. These are now not providing sufficient levels of protection as criminals develop ways to get around new technology.

ii. *Verified by Visa* and *MasterCard SecureCode*, allows the customer to set up a secure password for Internet transactions, to prevent criminals from using stolen cards.

iii. Retailers are also offered training and information how to prevent unauthorised card usage.

In addition retailers have internal policies, to set a maximum transaction value, if a purchase exceeded the threshold, then authorisation will be require from the bank to proceed with the transaction. Biometric technology could have a part to play in increasing security at ATM, but the technological problems and public resistance are the two major factors that are holding it back.

The Riverside Health Systems Employees Credit Union, introduced biometrics in 1998 and use fingerprint scan for identification that matches with information held on their database. The first time a customer uses a kiosk, they are asked for their account number and their fingerprint. The customer then shows a picture ID to an employee who then completes the registration process. The customer can also use their existing ATM card in the biometric kiosks, but if they choose to use the fingerprint reader they do not need to remember their PIN. More than 1000 of the credit unions 3200 customers have signed up for the scheme. Should the machine be unable to read a fingerprint, it suggests advice on how to improve the chances of a positive reading at the next attempt. Woori is one of the country's largest banking groups in South Korea introduced fingerprint technology at its ATM's throughout Korea, in an attempt to tighten up security of its customers banking transactions. The biometric information will also replace the use of passwords in authenticating customers doing transactions over the Internet (Mann P. 2004). So far the technology has only been applied in small financial institutions; if it is to become an international standard, questions about the security of the biometric data held by the institutions will have to be answered. *Will each bank keep its own database? Or should a third party operate the database?*

The Harrah casinos in the USA have installed ATM, which use facial recognition to replace the use of a PIN. At the first use the machine takes a photograph and gives you a receipt to take to the cashier. The cashier pulls your picture taken at the ACM up onto a screen; it is then checked against your photo ID. You are now enrolled onto the system, at future transactions the ACM takes a new photo, which is then checked with the information on the database, if there is a match you only need to type in how much cash you want. A San Francisco company is also using facial scans in its rapid pay machines (RPM) which not only act as cash dispensers but can also cash personal cheques, money orders and wire transfers. Our research shows that the companies that have so far embraced biometric technology have received positive feedback from their customers. Microsoft has committed itself to putting biometrics into a future release of Windows. Compaq computers have built a fingerprint scanner into the keyboard. Visa, MasterCard and Discover are doing pilots where fingerprints are put into the bar code, where the merchant puts the card into a reader, you place your finger on the reader and they know the card is yours.

In 2002, a number of German banks examined the feasibility of introducing biometrics into the ATM system; the decision was taken that for the foreseeable future biometrics would not be introduced at ATM's. The banks rejected biometrics on a number of counts. They, for example, did not consider biometrics to be appropriate for secure banking applications (such as ATMs) when large numbers of users are involved. Also the data and consumer protection requirements that are needed when using a biometric solution were seen as too complicated to integrate into existing procedures, especially considering there are still technical and handling problems to overcome with most biometric modalities. Another important reason to reject the use of biometrics at ATMs was not specifically related to the technology, but because of the difficulty in involving all national and international banking associations and bodies, which is necessary when introducing a new security system governing banking transactions.

The lack of standardisation and interoperability between the biometrics devices has hindered the easy deployment of most associated technologies, especially when combining them with existing systems. The immaturity of most systems in large scale applications; in terms of error rates and security requirements, also made it difficult to decide whether or not a system could fulfil the operators' needs. There is, of course, another practical problem that needs to be taken into account when using biometrics. The introduction of biometric authentication at ATMs is not simply a case of realising the possible benefits of biometrics. It means changing the entire security management process of the ATM system. Any advantages come at a high technical and organisational expense to the operator. The traditional ATM-card is posted to the customer in one envelope and the PIN in another, but the biometrics systems will only requires secure enrolment, which not only have to be undertaken by highly skilled personnel, but must ensure that person A does not enrol in place of person B.

Once enrolled in the system, people need to be re-enrolled after a certain time period. Aside from the expiry date on the ATM-card (typically after three years), the problem of biometric template ageing must also be considered, which means more customer maintenance than in traditional systems. In addition, comprehensive educational information about the biometric system covering issues, such as the storage and administration of biometric data, must be provided in a sensitive manner. This does not just mean providing general information at the time of enrolment into the system, but also to provide users with leaflets and contact points in case of system failure. When considering the legal technicalities of using biometrics in an ATM system, there are advantages that can be seen for consumers. Within the current system, the customer is usually the one who is blamed in the event of PIN or card misuse, due to contractual conditions and specific rules of evidence. With biometrics, the "negligent" handling of a biometric characteristic would not be a reasonable claim. It would not be admissible or socially acceptable for the customer to control their own biometric characteristic, such as their fingerprint left on a wineglass in a restaurant, or to avoid gardening because of possible injuries to their biometric. The responsibility to ensure that the biometric system cannot be forged and that replay attacks aren't successful would lie with the operator.

The operator would not be able to claim that the customer had acted negligently, and would have to ensure a high level of system security. Moreover, the bank would have to assume the burden of proof in the event of unauthorised access to a bank account via an ATM. In terms of privacy, both technical and organisational measures would have to maintained a high level of data security. Centralised data could, in theory, be accessible by criminals or law enforcement agencies, so there is a preference for decentralised storage. This would mean that verification of the individual is preferred to identification. In the ATM scenario, the preferred biometric would be used together with a token. Ideally the token, such as a smart card, would have on-card processing capabilities containing vital identity information. Another privacy issue relates to the concept of user consent. Before a bank's customer gives consent for their biometric to be used they must be comprehensively informed about the use of their biometric data, the measures taken to secure the data from misuse and forgery and other technical and organisational issues. From a legal standpoint, the boundaries for this voluntary consent would have to be clearly defined and only used for its intended purpose. This means that a bank is not allowed, for example, to share biometric data with other organisations if the customer had not given their prior consent.

According to Meridien Research Inc. in Newton, Mass., consumer fears and losses due to fraud are strong enough incentives for institutions to invest large sums of money in biometrics as an alternative to personal identification numbers. And with 500,000 cases of identity theft in the U.S. each year, consumers are ready to accept biometrics at the cost of decreased privacy and more intrusive methods of identification. Deutsche Bank AG in Frankfurt and New York based Citibank have been using biometrics for several years for employee access to computer server rooms. Citibank wants to be a leader in extending biometrics technology to customers, providing them with several identification options, such as fingerprint and facial recognition technologies, so they can choose the one with which they are most comfortable (Mearian, 2002). The biggest drawback to the introduction of biometric ATM's at the moment is money. Will the introduction save more money than the cost of implementing and maintaining the system? The systems also need to prove to be reliable in their ability to identify the user, and the customer should also have confidence that their biometric data is held securely.

8.3   Combined identity and verification

An independent regulator that is transparent in the use of biometric data would supervise the database. It will be inconvenient to members of the public if they have to repeatedly register their biometric details with different organisation. The biometric measured would be compared with the data held on the database and the card to confirmed the identity of the person. The details that each organisation can access will be restricted (based on the purpose and by who). This will prevent a bank from checking Mr A or Miss B medical report.

The biometric template is used to confirm the identity of a customer, cardholder or passport holder. Authorised access to the relevant database depends on the security procedures set up in the system; it should not compromise with wrong access. For example the police should only have access to the authorised database not otherwise (see Figures 3–11 for diagrammatic illustration).

Combining identity and verification of digital photograph, fingerprint, iris scan, signature and voice data would be enrolled into the 'National Biometric Database', and then accessed whenever a biometric measurements is submitted and needs to be verified. Many organisations will use the system to confirm individual's identity. We envision that the system dynamic will allow other organisations to join at a latter date. Different users will have different access rights.

9. OTHER AREAS OF APPLICATION

A basic criticism from the standpoint of privacy is that we, as individuals, lose our anonymity whenever biometric scanning systems are deployed. Controlling information about ourselves includes our ability to keep other parties from knowing who we are. In some cases, the benefits of establishing a person's identity outweigh the costs of losing anonymity. The following are cases in point where biometrics has enhanced security (Iridian Technologies, 2005):

9.1 Canada Customs and Revenue Agency

Canada Customs and Revenue Agency (CCRA) and Citizenship and Immigration Canada launched a pilot program called CANPASS-Air in September 2002 for the Canadian border. Iris recognition helps Canadian officials streamline airport operations while maintaining a safe and secure border. Iris recognition authenticates pre-approved, low-risk travellers who are citizens or permanent residents of the United States and Canada and clears them through "express lane" customs and immigration. The CANPASS-Air is operational at Pearson International Airport in Toronto, Vancouver, Calgary, Edmonton, Halifax, Montreal, Ottawa and Winnipeg. The hardware and software for CANPASS-Air is Iridian Proof Positive-certified, ensuring that the highest quality standards are met. All Iridian-certified iris recognition cameras meet US and international eye safety standards. Proof Positive-certification also guarantees scalability and full hardware and software interoperability, giving CCRA the option to extend the system with additional Proof Positive cameras or software in the future. The system has been extended to a bilateral system with the U.S.

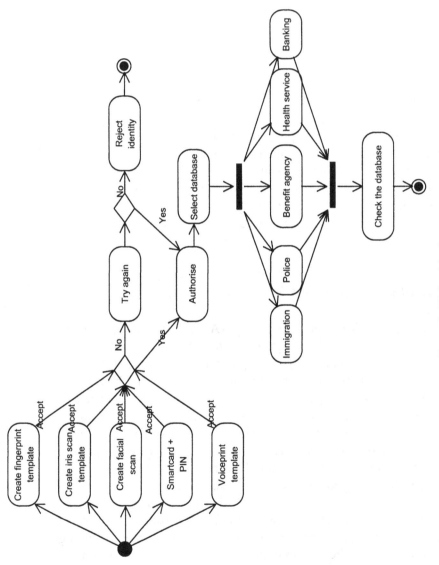

Figure 3–11. Combined system

9.2   JFK Airport, New York

A door to the tarmac of JFK Airport at Terminal 4, the international arrivals hall, was announced secured by the accuracy of iris recognition in November 2002. At the time of the announcement, 300 of the airport's 13,000 employees had already enrolled in a voluntary test program to prevent employee security breaches. To proceed through the door to the tarmac at Terminal 4 the employee's identification card must match a live read of the person's iris. If a card is presented, but the iris does not match the IrisCode® record for that person, the door to the tarmac will not open. In addition, physical security is dispatched to interview the individual and determine next steps, which may involve local authorities.

9.3   Schiphol Airport, The Netherlands

Starting in October, 2001, passengers in Schiphol Airport literally use their iris as their passport when their border control application performs a one-to-one verification between their "live" IrisCode® template and the one previously enrolled on their Privium smart card. Upon approval by the system, the individual is given rapid admission into or out of the country. In addition to an IrisCode template, the smart card contains passport data. Today, several thousand European Union (EU) passengers use iris recognition each day to bypass lengthy immigration and border control lines when entering or exiting the Netherlands. Border control officials concentrate manual passport examinations on unknown travellers, rather than "knowns" whose background checks reveal no security concerns.

9.4   United Nations, Pakistan and Congo

The first anonymous enrolment application was debuted in October 2002 when the United Nations High Commissioner for Refugees (UNHCR) began using iris recognition to enrol the IrisCode® template of Afghan refugees in Peshawar, Pakistan. As a part of this UN repatriation process, refugees are entitled to a one-time assistance package of travel funds and basic supplies. The system performs one-to-all identification fraud detection to ensure the refugee has not already been issued aid, thereby directing aid equitably to the entire population. Since the anonymous enrolment and fraud identification system has gone live, as many as 5,000 Afghani refugees per day have been processed with iris recognition. Numerous refugees who sought assistance multiple times have been detected as "recyclers," and in those cases, the aid has been re-directed to other needy recipients. In 2005, the UNHCR began to use this same system in The Congo.

9.5   Heathrow Airport, U.K.

In 2005, the UK installed "Project IRIS" in Heathrow airport as a fast lane for frequent travellers and visa holders. Four additional airports are yet to be added in 2006. On arrival into the United Kingdom, the enrolled passenger could approach an iris recognition kiosk and within seconds a one-to-many search against a database determined whether the patterns of his or her iris matched an IrisCode® record in the system. The system was designed to positively identify "known travellers" so that immigration and customs officials could focus their attention on examining unknown travellers.

9.6   Lancaster County Prison, Pennsylvania

A restricted access application based on iris recognition was installed in Lancaster County Prison in May 2001. Now, iris recognition technology controls physical access to the high security facility. All staff members are required to submit to a background check and enrol in the system to gain access, and over 1,000 regular visitors have also enrolled on a voluntary basis to speed up their admission into the prison. Iris recognition is also used in a separate application as a means to identify prison inmates at booking and release. There are many documented instances where iris recognition has prevented an inmate from perpetrating identity fraud.

9.7   Pentagon Officer's Athletic Club, Washington, D.C.

Military officers and Pentagon employees use iris recognition in identification mode for a restricted access application that secures the Pentagon's athletic club facilities. In addition to the one-to-all IrisCode® template search to confirm identity, a turnstile allows only one person through the main entrance at a time. A second remote optical unit is currently being installed at an outside entrance so that runners can also be authenticated. The system was integrated into a legacy card membership and accounting system. Iris recognition has successfully ensured that membership cards cannot be "loaned" for use by non-paying individuals who are not members of the club.

9.10   Narita Airport, Japan

In January 2003, Japan Airlines started a pilot program for simplified passenger travel at Narita Airport in Japan. The pilot is funded by the Japanese government and has enrolled 1,000 people in total for the study. The passenger service concept includes the use of a smart card with iris recognition for contact-less identification and to receive a ticket at check-in, pass through a security gate, and pass through the boarding gate. Four gates in all are enabled.

9.11   New Egypt Schools, New Jersey

In early 2003, iris recognition cameras were installed in three schools in the school district of Plumsted, NJ in an innovative program designed to improve school safety overall. New safety systems have been developed using the unparalleled accuracy of iris recognition technology to restrict access to the buildings and to establish the identity of both school employees and parents. The New Egypt Elementary School, Middle School and High School in Plumsted, NJ now use iris recognition to control who is admitted to the building after doors are locked at 9:00 am. School employees who are enrolled in the system have instant access when they glance at an iris recognition camera and the security software locates their unique iris image which has been previously stored in a database. Parents and other caregivers can also be enrolled in the system to streamline the process of picking up a child for early dismissal. The parent can confirm that they are authorised to retrieve the child by glancing into a camera located in the administration office.

9.12   Border Control, United Arab Emirates

The General Directorate of Abu Dhabi Police in the United Arab Emirates have installed iris recognition at land, sea and air border points. The project, which started in August 2001, involves the enrolment of inmates and expellees' irises from geographically distributed deportation centres throughout the UAE into a central iris database at the General Directorate of Abu Dhabi Police. A real-time, one-to-all, iris check of arriving passengers with new visit or work visas at any UAE border point will reveal if the person had been expelled from the country. The number of searches carried out to date has exceeded 7 million searches from land, sea and air border points, with a sustained real-time response reported by all sites on a 24x7 basis. The number of searches is expected to rise considerably in the next few months as the authorities will require more traveller categories to submit for an iris recognition at all UAE border entry points. The total number of enrolled IrisCode® templates of expelled persons has exceeded 900,000 records, the largest expellee IrisCode template database in the world. The system has already stopped more than 65,000 persons attempting to re-enter the country using passports with different names, some of the deportees had attempted to re-enter the country on the same day that they were expelled on.

9.13   City Hospital of Bad Reichenhall, Bavaria

In November 2002, an infant station in the City Hospital of Bad Reichenhall in Bavaria, Germany installed iris recognition to secure access and prevent baby abductions. This is the first time the technology has been used for infant protection, as it is more traditionally associated with border control and simplified passenger travel in airports. The secure entry system now permits only authorised people to gain access to the infant station. Authorised individuals include the mothers, nurses or doctors. These individuals enrol their iris in the system by glancing at an iris-recognition camera. In seconds, a unique IrisCode® template is generated that will later be matched against "live" samples of the iris whenever that person wants to enter the room. Once the child is released from the infant station, the mother's IrisCode® data is removed from the system and they are no longer allowed access.

9.14   University of South Alabama Hospitals, Alabama

An innovative iris recognition-enabled medical records management solution was launched at University of South Alabama (USA) Hospitals in Mobile, AL in July 2002. Iris authentication replaces user ID and password access to the CARLOS (Computer Aided Record Location and Deficiency Systems) systems at the three USA Hospitals, including Women's and Children's, Medical Center and Knollwood. With iris recognition technology, only clinicians with appropriate access privileges are granted permission to view information and associated reports. The new system keeps sensitive clinical information secured from inappropriate access. These improvements are part of the University of South Alabama's strategy for compliance with the Health Insurance Portability and Accountability Act (HIPAA).

9.15   Eagleville Hospital, Pennsylvania

Eagleville Hospital, Eagleville, PA installed its Politec Authentication Security Suite (PASS) in March 2002 using iris recognition biometric technology to strengthen system security in preparation for the data privacy and computer security requirements of the Health Insurance Portability and Accountability Act (HIPAA). The PASS system is a complete, robust security solution that is used to secure, manage and control access to electronic information and can also be used to secure physical environments. This flexible system enables assignment and administration of roles, responsibilities, policies and procedures for each individual user from a central location. Iris recognition is used to authenticate their identity, dramatically improving on password and PIN-based information technology security.

9.16   Transaction Security

Bank of Central Asia (BCA), Indonesia, uses biometrics to protect the interests of their customers; staff and the bank by ensuring that only authorised personnel handle bank transactions. Existing methods of authorising transactions by the bank's tellers and supervisors through the use of PINs and passwords could be open to fraud and misuse. Replacing traditional passwords, Identix' biometric system verifies the identity of employees who authorise withdrawals, deposits and electronic transfers over a certain amount and records an irrefutable audit trail. BCA has deployed Identix technology in more than 700 branches throughout Indonesia. The Bank of Cairo is installing a similar system to that used by BCA. To date some 1,000 units have been put into operation.

9.17   ATM Security and Monitoring

Armaguard Australia, a division of Mayne Nickless Ltd, and one of the world's largest cash transport companies, was the first company to use portable biometric devices from Identix. These devices are now installed on the cash security door of over 2,000 ATMs across Australia. The guards, who replenish and service the ATMs, carry a portable sensor with them, which is used to verify identity and open the cash security door. An irrefutable electronic audit trail is created, recording who was biometrically verified both at the time of opening and the time of closing the ATM while the ATM is being refilled with money or being serviced. All communication with the ATMs is done remotely using Identix software. In the seven years Armaguard was using Identix' biometric devices, there has not been one major theft of an ATM protected by Identix fingerprint technology.

9.18   Customer Passbook Identification

Conavi Bank of Medellin in Colombia uses Identix biometric devices to irrefutably identify "passbook" account customers at each branch. Previous methods, which involved comparing signatures against microfiche records, were slow and insecure – in the event of fraud, the liability lay with the customer. Conavi saw the biometric solution as a unique competitive advantage as well as offering a genuine benefit to its customers.

9.19   Bank Vault Access

The People's Bank of China has installed over 150 Identix access control units to provide added security to the bank's vaults throughout the country.

9.20   Secure Member-Bank Database Access

To ensure the unfettered exchange of sensitive data and information without risking unauthorised access, the Central Bank of Costa Rica has deployed Identix fingerprint security solutions to secure access to its databases by member banks. The Banco Central de Costa Rica ensures that only authorised officers from its recognised member banks can access the Central Bank's databases by requiring verification through fingerprint biometrics prior to allowing access. The Central Bank has deployed more than 400 Identix BioTouch USB fingerprint readers to its network of member banks and has also purchased a BioLogon server license to enable up to 1,000 users to enroll in the new security system.

9.21   Asset Protection and Remote Banking

Colombia Bancafe, a large government-owned bank in Colombia with over 2 million clients in over 400 branches, uses Identix fingerprint biometrics to provide customers with a higher level of security for their transactions in a faster and safer way, and without the hassle of passwords or PINs. The application uses fingerprint technology for customer verification at the teller as well as in the bank's ATM network. According to the bank, customers have noticed the faster service they get when doing business over the counter or through the ATM with biometrics. As a result of the success, Bancafe has used biometrics as a marketing tool to attract customers that may be concerned about identity fraud and the security of their assets.

9.22 Customer Touchpoints and Remote Banking

Chile-based Banco Falabella has adopted biometric banking for its branches throughout the country. The bank has integrated Identix biometric security solutions to provide heightened security for its customers, while eliminating the need to remember cumbersome passwords. Customers are required to verify their identity via the fingerprint readers prior to performing a transaction with a teller. The bank has also installed Identix technology at its credit card centers to verify customer identification prior to making a withdrawal on a card. Finally, the bank has integrated Identix biometrics into select ATMs to replace PIN numbers for customer withdrawals.

Transaction Verification for Commodities Traders

The Brazilian Mercantile & Futures Exchange (BM&F) is the world's first stock market to implement fingerprint biometrics security for authentication and access to its electronic Global Trading System. The solution requires traders to access the electronic Global Trading System via fingerprint biometric authentication. Traders are required to verity their identity via the fingerprint readers periodically at defined time intervals throughout the period of time they are logged-on to the system. This helps to guarantee the security and exclusiveness of access by authorised traders to the electronic Global Trading System by verifying that an individual placing a trade was actually the one authorised to make the trade.

Other areas of biometrics application and implementations are discussed in chapter 4.

10.   SUMMARY OF CHAPTER THREE

Incorporating biometrics into existing systems may be difficult, if the system is not planned in advance. Compatibility problems between databases and hardware devices must be resolved through the implementation of international standards. The system must also be given the capacity and the resources to deal with millions of expected requests. The next chapter focuses on the methodology adopted and presents the Shoniregun and Crosier Secured Biometrics Applications Model (SCSBAM).

REFERENCES

Atos, 2005, *UK Passport Service Biometrics Enrolment Trial, Management Summary*, UK Passport Service, May.

Cardwatch., 2005, *Card Fraud Overview*, http://www.cardwatch.org.uk/default.asp ?sectionid=5&pageid =82, (November 11, 2006).

Davies S.G., 1994, 'Touching Big Brother – How Biometric Technology Will Fuse Flesh and Machine', *Information Technology and People*, Volume 7, No 4, 1994, pp 38-47, MCB University Press 0959-3845

Horizon, 2005, *Making Millions the Easy Way*, BBC-Science -Horizon, http://www.bbc.co.uk/sn/tvradio/programmes/horizon/million_trans.shtml, (November 21, 2006).

ICAO TAG MRTD/NTWG., 2004, *Biometric Deployment of Machine Readable Passports –Technical Report*, International Civil Aviation Authority, (March 6 2007).

Ingram, B., 1999, *Fingering a new checkout technology*, Supermarket Business, Oct 15, Volume 54, Issue 10.

Iridian Technologies, 2005, *Selected case studies*, http://www.iridiantech.com/solutio ons.php?page=2, (March 21, 2007).

Jain A.K. et al., 1998, *Biometric Based Web Access*, MSU Technical Report, http://biometrics.cse.msu.edu/publications.html, (January 1, 2006).

Krawczyk S. Jain A.K.2005, 'Securing Electronic Records using Biometric Authentication', *Proceedings of the Audio- and Video-Based Biometric Person Authentication (AVBPA 2005)*, pp 1110-1119, Rye Brook, NY, http://www.biometrics.cse.msu.edu/publications.html (August 2, 2007).

Mann P., 2004, 'Woori Bank Deploys Biometrics at ATMs', *Biometric Technology Today*, September.

Mearian, L., 2002, 'Banks eye biometrics to deter consumer fraud', *Computerworld*, Jan 28, 2002, Volume 36, Issue 5.

Rejman-Greene, M. 2003, 'A framework for the development of biometric systems', *Biometric Technology Today*, Volume 11, Issue 1, January 2003.

Rragami L., Edwards N.H., 2003, 'Securing Web Services with Biometrics', *Business Technology Today*, May 2003 Volume 11, Issue 5.

Shoniregun, C, A., 2005, *Impacts and Risk Assessment of Technology for Internet Security: Enabled Information Small-Medium Enterprises (TEISMES)*, Springer, New York, USA.

Chapter 4

SECURING BIOMETRICS APPLICATIONS

1. INTRODUCTION

The biometrics techniques are developed to provide increased security features in computers systems, passports, identity cards, credit cards, organisation's systems, and entry to government departments but now there has never been a proposed model on how best biometrics applications can be secured. The main biometric measures are fingerprints, palm, retinal scans, keystroke, voice recognition and facial scanning. To avoid people having to submit their biometric details on a number of occasions for different purposes, we are proposing that the biometric information should be based on the national ID card or centralised Passport database systems. Once a person has registered they can offer their permission to the bank to use their biometric data to validate transactions.

Can biometric applications be secured?

—Charles Shoniregun, ECAI 2007, Keynote address.

The biggest concern is with the governments and large corporations having control of large amounts of personal data. The public do not have confidence in how this information is likely to be used, so appropriate measures will need to be taken to give the public confidence in the security and integrity of the information storage and management of the database systems. This chapter presents the results of the case studies, laboratory experiments, and Shoniregun and Crosier Secured Biometrics Applications Model (SBAM).

2.   METHODS AND METHODOLOGY

To identify appropriate research methods for this research, the taxonomy of Information Systems research methods proposed by Galliers (1992) was adopted. In this taxonomy he adequately combined research methods. This chapter focuses on the methodology adopted in attaining the data and/or information required to prove or disprove the stated hypothesises in chapter 1. The Shoniregun and Crosier Secure Biometrics Applications (SCSBA) Model is proposed in this chapter.

The methodology by any study must be appropriate for the objectives of that study. The scientific methodology is a system of explicit rules and procedures on which research is based and against which claims for knowledge are evaluated. The methodology used within the framework of this study are bound and based on a combination of the following:

- Formal theory

- Case studies

- Laboratory experiments

This study opts for all of the above options, hence it is propounded that research without methodology is like a ship without a captain. The use of formal theory, case studies and laboratory experiments are the primary methods of data collection and information gathering for the purpose of satisfying the hypothesis.

3.   CASE STUDIES

The term case study has multiple meanings. It can be used to describe a unit of analysis (e.g. a case study of particular business), or to describe a method. A case study approach is considered valid for this research. Benbasat *et al.*, (1987)) and Yin (1994 discusses the merits of using multiple case studies to provide replication logic and rich descriptions of emergent research areas. Multiple case study analysis has been justified and validated by researchers such as Zikmund (1997), who investigated inter organisation systems. For the purpose of brevity, case studies representative of the different biometrics adaptations and applications were study. The following case studies highlight the use of biometrics in a variety of applications from employee background checking, ID card, point of sale ID verification, and remote banking. In all cases, it should be noted that biometrics are a part of the solution:

3.1   Expelles tracking and border control system in UAE

It was discovered that foreigners expelled from the United Arab Emirate (UAE) change their name and perhaps their nationality and are therefore issued a different passport in a different name. Reports by the UAE police showed that traditional computer list depends on name, date of birth and so information can be changed after expulsion: can individuals come back under a different name and nationality? The Government of UAE contracted Iridian technologies Inc to install an iris biometric system. The biometric was used to scan incoming arrivals (with new visas) to tell if they have been expelled before.

The project started in august 2001, which involves the enrolment of inmates and expellees' irises from geographically distributed prisons and deportation centres throughout the UAE into a central iris database. Then a real-time, one-to-all, iris check of all arriving passengers at any UAE border point is done to reveal if the person has been expelled from the country. The pilot program was rolled out between June 2001 to October 2002 (18 months) in which 3 enrolment centres were installed in prison and deportation centre and from October to December 2002, it was installed in three recognition centres all connected to the central database. The national rollout was between January and April 2003, so far people from more than 152 nationalities have been scanned, more than 5,973,208 searches have been made, more than 2,000,000,000,000 cross comparison have been done and an average of more than 9,000 searches are done per day with an average of 90-95 persons being caught daily and according to report by Souza (2006), 50,452 persons have been caught and not allowed to enter UAE as of October 2005. Also there have not been any false matches yet, and over 6,800,000 people have used it so far without a single Failure to Enrol Rate (Souza (2006), Al Itihab newspaper (2004)).

3.2   Medicaid fraud and abuse detection system

Texas Medicaid Program is a Federal – state funded medical program that pays for the medical care for the poor. It is the largest source of funding for medical and health related services for America's poorest. This involves being issued a card for identification in which the client will show before medical service is rendered. However, because of lack of adequate security a lot of people were able to circumvent the system to use it. Ineligible individuals were able to use an eligible person's medical card to receive the services, services providers were able to claim services that were not rendered (also called phantom billing) or they claim more than the services they rendered, thereby incurring additional cost for the government. In 1998, the Texas health and human services commission (HHSC), implemented the medical fraud and abuse detection system (MFADS) with the aim of:

- Reducing the total amount of Medicaid expenditures wasted on fraud and abuse.

- Reducing "Phantom Billing" within the Medicaid system.

- Stopping client medicard ID sharing and card swapping.

Medicaid clients were issued smart cards stored with a digital representation of their fingerprint, in which at the time of service, the provider will insert the client's card into a point-of-service device to access the data on the card. The client then places their finger on a biometric device to be validated. Then the client will proceed with normal medical service and upon completion of the medical service, the client checks out using the same procedure, thereby creating a service visit duration time stamp. This information is transmitted to the state and is ultimately compared to the bill prepared by the service provider and submitted to the Medicaid office for payment.

The use of fingerprint for the program has been able to

- Deter fraudulent activity on the part of providers and clients.

- Alert providers in cases of potential misuse on the part of a client before services are rendered.

- Reduce total amount of Medicaid fraud cases arising from authentication fraud and abuse.

- Reduce the total amount of Medicaid expenditures by generating substantial, measurable and sustainable cost saving for taxpayers' money.

- Reduced the number of fraudulent participants in the Medicaid program.

Petraborg and Scott (2006) reported that the state of Texas has saved approximately $11 million by the implementation of this program.

3.3   Gladestone House (Lasch)

Gladestone house is a local authority secure children home based in Liverpool, UK focusing on attending to the physical, emotional and behavioural needs of the young people they accommodate. It accommodates young offenders aged 12 – 16 for girls and 15 – 16 for boys who are assessed to be vulnerable. It has 80 members of staff and accommodates 18 young people. The keys should never leave the building premises, so this requires staff at the beginning and at the end of their shift to be escorted in and out of the facility. However, a cost benefit analysis of this process was carried out by the management at Gladestone house and it was discovered that around 35 man hours per week which creates an annual overhead of £18,000, and the process also presents a potential security threat, given that anyone in possession of the key could potentially gain access. The Gladstone house management recognised that the hand geometry recognition can facilitate access to the secure unit while at the same time enhances the security at key access points. The hand geometry recognition system was installed to grant access to authorised persons upon presentation of their hand to the hand geometry reader. This has replaced the key and has stopped the problem of needing the assistance of a colleague to get in and out of the facility. Also, apart from the security of not having the key fall into the wrong hands, the system can also capture the attendance level and time for each employee who provides visibility and accuracy of data that was not previously possible. According to Gladstone house building the new system will enhance security, facilitates a simpler and more convenient process for staff.

3.4   CrimTrac

In the late 1980s the Australian government implemented a National Automated Fingerprint Identification System (NAFIS), by the late 1990s the system had run out of capacity. It is a must that the system should be enhanced with advanced biometric technology. In mid-2000 the Australian Government established CrimTrac, a national crime agency with a mandate to develop the four key information systems:

• National Automated Fingerprint Identification System (NAFIS),

- National criminal DNA database,

- National child sex offender system, and

- Rapid access to the national operational policing data (Crimtrac Police Reference System – CPRS).

The CrimTrac selected SAGEM to design, implement and maintain the NAFIS after converting the existing paper fingerprint forms and unsolved latent records (alphanumeric data and minutiae maps) retrieved from the existing NEC system. The NAFIS became operational in April 2001. The CrimTrac NAFIS holds the largest automated palm print database in the world. The system has been required to keep up with a NAFIS throughput that has significantly exceeded expectations in 2003. The heavy usage of NAFIS by police agencies is confirmed by the monthly throughput figures: an average of 12,500 crime scene latent searches and approximately 10% identification confirmed. The CrimTrac NAFIS training and test environment was also a big help to Indonesian and Australian Government for the identification of the victims of the Bali bombing. The NAFIS implementation was a significant accomplishment both technically and geographically. The CrimTrac NAFIS has become an advertisement for the integration of fingerprint and palm print system that every police agency worldwide would like to have.

3.5   Precise Biometrics

The Schools in Stockholm Stad (City of Stockholm, Sweden), consisting of 170 individual schools and a total of 80,000 Novell network users, starting their computer education in the first grade and continue using computers through high school. Initially 450 users at the Kvarnby School were provided with biometrics. Although the Kvarnby School in Stockholm had come a long way when it comes to IT, the school still suffered from password administration problems. While younger students found it difficult to remember passwords, older students occasionally borrowed user names and passwords belonging to other students and, for example, accessed unapproved websites from the computer lab. In addition, the school needed to find an easy-to-use solution that saved classroom time and could be installed, operated and maintained without becoming a major drain on the school's budget. At the beginning of the test, Precise Biometrics had problems because the children's fingers were too small for the readers. They simply did not contain enough information. But after going back to the drawing board, Precise Biometrics came back with a matching method specially adapted for children's fingers.

After extensive research, the IT group decided that a fingerprint based solution for login would eliminate the identification problems. Precise Biometrics distributor was adopted for providing login solution at the Kvarnby School and made it possible for the IT administrators to be sure that people were who they claimed to be. Students did not have to remember passwords any longer, or worry about someone misusing their login ID. With the fingerprint readers in place at the Kvarnby School's workstations, problems with forgotten or misused passwords have practically been eliminated. Now all 450 students and teachers are logging on to the computers using their fingerprint, which has not only made the login routines easier, but also saves valuable classroom time— up to 50% on a 40 min lesson. Other schools within the Stockholm school system are now considering implementing the same fulfilling solution.

The Precise Biometrics works on both USB ports and parallel ports. It is cost effective solution that can be easily integrated in the client's current environment, and solved the school's identification issues. When Stockholm municipality chose the Kvarnby School to test fingerprint readers in a pilot project two years ago, it was because the school already had a very advanced IT program. The system identifies individual's biometrics profile not passwords. On average, half of the lesson time would pass before teachers could help children sort out their passwords. They frequently had to go to the network administrator to change their passwords. It went so far that the children's passwords were written up on the blackboard in the classroom. Children sometimes bullied the younger ones into giving up their passwords and had unauthorized access to the computers. "With the fingerprint readers all the problems disappeared. It was much better from a security perspective and saved teaching time". The system has saved classroom time and reduced costs. It was also considerably easier for the children. They sit down at the computers, type their login, which is based on their names, and put their left index finger on the reader beside the keyboard. The children's fingerprints have been pre-registered by the network administrator during enrollment.

3.6 Bornholmstrafikken

Every year 1.2 million passengers cross the waters between the Danish island Bornholm and the Danish and Swedish mainland with the Bornholmstrafikken ferries. A substantial part of the passengers are commuters. The Bornholmstrafikken struggled with long lines at the ticket sales and suffered from high costs for administration of ticket sales and check-in. While the group of commuters among the customers had to stand in time-consuming lines, costs for ticket administration were unreasonably high. The Bornholmstrafikken shipping company needed to find an easy-to-use solution that could be installed, operated and maintained within the margins for budget.

The Precise Biometrics' partner PayVend Solutions, a Danish systems integrator and distributor of payment systems were contacted by Bornholmstrafikken, they decided a solution based on the combination of fingerprints and cards would solve the ticket sales queue. Less time could then be spent on administration and passengers could handle the purchase of tickets and check-in themselves, without having to spend time in lines. In addition, the administrators would know exactly who boarded the ferry. After installing the fingerprint-based solution at all of Bornholmstrafikkens ferry-stations in Denmark and Sweden, Bornholmstrafikken expects to increase the customers' service. The idea of using fingerprints came up after hearing about SAS Airlines testing Precise Biometrics' technology for checking-in passengers at aircraft. Precise Biometrics' fingerprint technology was integrated into the Pay Vend Solutions payment system, and Bornholmstrafikken was offered an easy-to-use system that met their demands for decreased administration costs and user convenience. Quick and secure, are some of the comments on the new ticket and check-in system for commuters at Bornholmstrafikken, provided by Precise Biometrics and its Danish partner, the systems integrator PayVend Solutions. The new system for the estimated 10,000 frequent travellers at Bornholmstrafikken was introduced at the beginning of year 2003 and gives the passengers the possibility to handle the purchase of tickets and check-in themselves, using a smart card and their fingerprint.

The commuters can now book their tickets in advance either through a booking system on the Internet or by telephone. When passengers arrive at the ferry-station, all they have to do is put their smart card and fingerprint on one of the fingerprint readers to confirm their reservation and then board the ferry. The former system was characterized by long-winded and time-consuming procedures as passengers had to stand in line to get the discounted tickets they were entitled to, as well as for check-in. The cardholder is the only one who can use the card, as it cannot be used without the cardholder "unlocking" it with his or her fingerprint. However, in addition to saving time, the usage of fingerprints also means increased security. The majority of the passengers welcomed the idea of a new ticket and check in system but there are still concerns over personal integrity.

3.7   BIO-key INS Pass

The government is attempting to reduce our vulnerability to terrorist incidents by increasing security at airports, border crossings and related facilities. To illustrate the exceptional security that biometric fingerprint identification can provide; BIO-key™ International introduces the INS Pass Demo System, a case study demonstration in biometric access for National security, showing 'True User Identification™'. The BIO-key's automated finger identification provides security and the technology use INS Pass. The INS Pass processes immigrant identification transactions, and performs verification for entry or exit approval. In order to guarantee an immigrant's identification, it employs WEB-key, BIO-key's Web-based VST finger identification solution. The BIO-key demonstration shows an effective INS Pass security system using BIO-key's advanced biometric identification technology:

- On submission of fingerprints by an immigrant for obtaining a Visa or at the point of entry into the country — the identification, the image created by the reader is converted into a mathematical model.

- The immigrant's finger model and Visa information are sent to the INS Pass server, protected by encryption, and the identification routine is initiated. The VST algorithm compares the immigrant's finger model against potentially millions of other individual's finger models.

- If a match is found, the finger model provides the "key" to the immigrant's profile information and either issues an approval or denies the right to enter/exit.

- After comparing the immigrant profile, the server sends confirmation back to the INS officer and allows further processing.

The identification steps are completed in only a few seconds, providing more security and convenience in less time. The system incorporates the biometric enrollment of immigrants as part of Visa acquisition, identifies them to gain an entry pass, and then verifies their identity as they enter the country. The same system also monitors employee access to facilities and systems and all transactions with immigrants. The INS processes the BIO-key solution of how an identity and validity check of foreign nationals could occur, and flags suspected and known criminals before they enter, or leave. The personal privacy of using BIO-key technology is that it prevents others from using our identities to commit crimes or other actions against us, or others, by using our identities.

3.8   Purdue Federal Employees Credit Union

The Indiana's Purdue Employees Federal Credit Union (PEFCU) at West Lafayette faced a substantial challenge in the late 1990s as it looked to offer banking services to members on remote campuses of Purdue University. The PEFCU planned to deploy kiosks at these locations in order to avoid the prohibitive expense of opening a brick-and-mortar branch on each campus. At the time, kiosks were convenient, but had significant limitations. Like most credit unions, the PEFCU was extremely sensitive to ensuring the best possible banking experience for its members. Automated kiosks are an important customer tool for credit unions and other financial institutions, providing a cost effective method for extending and expanding service locations and hours of operation. These kiosks, however, came with their own set of challenges, as it was difficult to remotely and securely offer a broad range of financial services beyond the simple deposit/withdrawal functions of a basic ATM. This limited the effectiveness of kiosks – a traditional brick-and-mortar presence was required for any sort of significant interaction between a customer and the financial institution. This was expensive for the institution and inconvenient for the customer.

In 1998, existing ATMs and kiosks were not ideal locations for customers to open an account – new members would have to wait 3-5 days to access funds or perform additional transactions. The delay was due to the need to process a transaction and physically mail a new ATM access card and PIN. For a credit union priding itself on customer service, this sort of delay was unacceptable. In addition, the type of transactions that could be performed at a typical ATM was limited by the need to absolutely verify and authenticate the account holder for complex services or high-value transactions. Taken together, these two considerations explain the service limitations of ATMs today and highlight the difficulty faced by an institution looking to leverage kiosks to expand its service network. Fortunately for the PEFCU, there was an answer: biometrics. By incorporating biometric technology (specifically, fingerprint recognition) into its kiosks, the PEFCU is now able to initiate accounts instantaneously. A new customer's fingerprint effectively became his or her personal ATM card, for use at any the PEFCU kiosk. In short, kiosks can now serve as branch offices, providing rapid and straightforward self-service banking. From the customers' perspective, this not only makes the PEFCU more accessible, but it also dramatically improves the convenience of accessing their accounts and performing complex transactions. It is now possible to bank 24 hours a day, seven days a week. For a credit union dedicated to meeting the banking needs of a university population and their unpredictable schedule – this was a critical win. For the PEFCU, biometric kiosks are also a business revelation. The credit union can now offer services in remote locations that would be cost-prohibitive for traditional branch offices. The PEFCU can also use kiosks to service the majority of customer banking needs – further improving overall customer service – and freeing credit union staff to deal with more complex banking requirements.

In 1998, the PEFCU selected kiosks from manufacturer Real-time Data (RTD) and a biometric authentication system from SAFLINK. SAFLINK's software provided a robust platform for tightly coupling biometrics with the complex kiosk software, and SAFLINK worked closely with both PEFCU and RTD to ensure the completed solution met the credit union's expectations. The credit union chose to perform a test installation at a branch on the main Purdue campus so that it could closely monitor the deployment. This test period went smoothly, and standalone kiosks were quickly deployed to remote campuses. In fact, the overall customer reaction to the new kiosks was so enthusiastic that PEFCU chose to expand the deployment with additional kiosk locations near the main Purdue University campus. One interesting development occurred during the early phases of the initial deployment. The PEFCU assumed that the kiosks and biometric security features would primarily appeal to the University's student population, reflecting their greater comfort with new technology. While the students did embrace the technology, one of the primary beneficiaries turned out to be the credit union's older membership. These customers were more sensitive to the problem of fraud and identity theft and had a substantially larger asset base to protect – making the heightened security of biometrics especially attractive. The PEFCU was the first financial institution in the country to incorporate biometrics-based authentication into its customer banking system. Biometrics proved to be so successful for the PEFCU:

•   Secure kiosks have now been online and reliable for five years

•   Credit union is now in the process of expanding its use of biometrics to its internal network.

The driving element for this internal deployment was a need for two-factor authentication for PEFCU employees with remote access to internal systems. The credit union had previously deployed Citrix MetaFrame XP to provide remote, password-based access for employees. One of the credit union's routine procedural audits noted the weakness of this single-factor login method and recommended an increase in their level of authentication security. After an extensive product evaluation the PEFCU chose SAFLINK's SAFremote Authenticator™ and has rolled this product out for remote Citrix users with the help of Roeing Corporation, a systems integrator. Since the initial experience with SAFLINK's software there has been a growing confidence in selecting SAFremote Authenticator product for use within the PEFCU's internal network.

In fact, the credit union has been so pleased with this solution that it is in the process of rolling out a more extensive biometric security solution for all employees – not just remote users. Through the kiosk deployment, the PEFCU has learned that a fingerprint is much more convenient for the customers than a PIN or ATM card, and it is more secure. Today, PEFCU has grown to proudly serve more than 56,000 members around the world, and is known for implementing leading-edge technology in its IT and banking systems.

3.9   FaceIt

In fulfilment of the mandate put forth to enhanced border security and the Visa Entry Reform Act, the US Department of State has chosen facial recognition technology for screening against duplicates and aliases prior to issuing a visa. After the cost evaluation of the project, the latest version of the Identix ABIS™ system powered by the company's state-of-the-art FaceIt® technology was agreed upon to be the technology of the future for the US Department of State. The Identix FaceIt technology is based on the combination of a leading local feature analysis (LFA) algorithm and skin biometrics for maximum accuracy, and has been validated in independent government evaluations. The FaceIt technology has been deployed worldwide in government, commercial and law enforcement applications. The Identix ABIS system allows unlimited scalability in terms of database size, throughput and response time, and incorporates an image quality control module to ensure high performance down the line. This system will also process the ten million applicants for e-Diversity visas each year (the e-Diversity visa program applies to applicants from countries with low levels of immigration to the US). Under this classification, applicants are allowed to obtain permanent residence visas.

The initial enrolment will include 35 million legacy visa images. In addition, an estimated eight million new visa images are expected to be enrolled over the next five years. The system is designed to match up to 2,000 facial images per hour and has built-in fail over protection to ensure 24/7 continuous operations. The Identix ABIS System is an advanced multi-biometric search engine designed for developing large-scale, one-to-many systems, with specific applicability to end user ID programs such as Passport and Visa issuance, National IDs, DMVs and large-scale enterprise employee ID issuance and verification.

3.10   Bowling Center Strikes

Before the biometric HandPunch, it took about three hours to calculate payroll manually but with biometric HandPunch the entire payroll is done in 15 minutes. All nine locales of the Don Carter All Star Lanes are in three different states. They are now using biometric HandPunch terminals to clock its 700 employees in and out, saving the corporation between 400 to 500 hours of payroll preparation time per year.

The biometric HandPunch eliminates the expenses associated with employee badges and fraud caused by buddy punching. Instead of having to fill out or punch timecards, employees simply place their hands on the biometric HandPunch device. It automatically takes a three-dimensional reading of the size and shape of the employee's hand and verifies the user's identity in less than one second. Each employee has his/her own code, which is keyed into the HandPunch. They then present their hand to the HandPunch and are clocked into work. Upon leaving work, they repeat the process. With the Gatekeeper Business Solutions software, managers at each location create the database and then upload the information to the corporate office where the payroll is run.

The biometric HandPunch assures the person checking in is physically there. That eliminates buddy punching. The device units interface with Gatekeeper Business Solutions software. The Gatekeeper Business Solutions provides a high tech hardware and software solution for Don Carter All Star Lanes to aggressively reduce labour expense and to automate the time and attendance and payroll processes. It is now possible to merge punches, produce a time attendance report, run overtime reports and analyse data quickly.

3.11   HandKey Tightens Security for Anaheim's Arrowhead Pond

The Arrowhead Pond, a premier Southern California entertainment and sports venue and home of the NHL Anaheim Mighty Ducks, is using a HandKey® hand geometry reader to protect access to the complex. Hand geometry readers positively identify users by the shape and size of their hands, not their keys, cards or codes. Prior to the HandKey the magnetic stripe card-based system was in use but people were simply handing their cards off to friends, letting them in for free. Needless, this was creating problems and the security was lax, so an alternative solution system that provided greater security through better identification is required. The Pond looked at several alternatives, including other biometric technologies, but found them too expensive. The HandKey was installed in early September of 2001 at the Southeast entrance to the building, where the majority of employees report for duty, just off the administrative offices and the Mighty Ducks locker room. Whether an All Star winger or sales manager, an employee enters a four-digit pin code on the HandKey and swoops a hand into the reader, which then compares the hand's length, width, thickness and surface area with the template stored in the unit. The process takes approximately one second and is virtually foolproof. When a match occurs, the door opens.

The hand reader has tightened access into the Pond. Two people in administration can access the system and make changes from their desktop PCs. When someone leaves the organisation, Pond administrators quickly and easily delete that user's record with a couple of clicks and block any further entrance to the Pond.

3.12   Analysis of case studies

The analysis of the case studies shows that at all points in time the adaptors of biometrics technologies were combining biometrics with a generic security approach. It was also noted that only single biometric identification is in use in most cases, this should not be so, because a single biometric identification is a failure without a combination of a number of individual biometrics profile (see chapter 2, section 4 and SCSBA model). It is apparent that there is no centralised database system in operation, which makes individual cases questionable in terms of privacy and the legitimacy of how the biometrics profiles are been used. A centralised system is likely to be very strictly governed and regulated therefore biometrics security is complementary to generic security approach when it is centralised.

4. CLASSIFICATIONS AND TAXONOMY OF BIOMETRICS APPLICATIONS

The classification and taxonomy of biometrics are based on historical paradigm. Over the past few years, we have seen evidence of an increasing number of individual biometrics profiles used in both commercial and government sectors with wider area of implementations. Research has shown that there has never been a classification and taxonomy of biometrics; therefore, the first proposition of biometrics classification and taxonomy is based on the past and presents applicability (see Table 4-1).

Table 4–1. Classification and taxonomy of biometrics

Types of biometrics	Purpose	Enhance security
Regressive biometrics	Punishments	Negative (–)
Progressive biometrics	Security Measures	Positive (+)

i. Regressive biometrics

The regressive biometrics can be traced back to the ancient Roman, when thieves are punished for an offence committed against individuals or state. The usual punishment ranges from cutting the criminal's finger(s), toe(s), leg(s), ear(s), and removing their eye(s). Although these are barbaric acts that should not have been encouraged, however, it has also been noted that some countries still uses regressive biometrics as away of punishing criminals. The countries that have such punishments carry them out in isolation because of the international human right laws. The regressive biometrics is also referred to as capital punishment.

ii. Progressive biometrics

The introduction of progressive biometrics in computers and mobile devices has opened a market trend for other technologies to embrace biometrics applications. The progressive biometrics is becoming increasingly popular for future security systems worldwide. Unlike regressive biometrics, the progressive biometrics are sophisticated security measures. It is used as modern day sophisticated security measures.

It was the terrorists' invasion; individual privacy and government border control has led to the adoption of full-scale biometrics. The ability to enhance the existing systems security breaches within and outside the controlled boundary requires access control and remote access control. To make existing systems more secured against password breaches, it is believed that individual biometrics can be used to enhance systems security, that is, if individual biometrics cannot be duplicated but the facts remains that no system can 100 percent secured. Therefore enhancing security of any systems requires an incremental approach that can be enhanced with combined biometrics profiles. Safe and secured biometrics system should have the following characteristics:

- The system is connected to another super systems or similar systems with all the integral parts working accordingly to expectation. All other subsystems are fully aware of their own function.

- All the connected systems are free from human interventions. The reason for this is that human interaction is likely to pollute the systems to malfunction. For example, introducing a command that will perform illegal operations.

- The system should only be interacting with, if and only when repair is required, which should be under strict security.

However, the ideology about safe and secured systems is very hypothetical, which is open to many interpretations.

Hypothesis 1:

- Null hypothesis (H_0^1): Classification and taxonomy of biometrics are unattainable.

- Alternative (H_A^1): Classification and taxonomy of biometrics are attainable.

Outcome of Hypothesis 1

- (H_0^1) is rejected in favour of (H_A^1)

- As a result of the investigation classification and taxonomy of biometrics are attainable.

5. LABORATORY TEST

We initially conducted laboratory experiments on 5 top biometrics manufacturers products to see the capability of the in-built resilient (we try not to list the names of the biometrics manufacturers for privacy reasons). The great majority of the currently available biometrics products rely on features of the fingers for user identification, face recognition and iris scanning systems. All other devices and programs that use language recognition, hand geometry measurement, signature recognition or keyboard touch dynamics have a marginal share of the security biometrics industry. The marketing opportunities for facial feature recognition devices and programs are assumed to be fairly good. We need to emphasise that all manufacturers' statements, have said that none of the products tested by us was designed for use in a high-security environment. Nevertheless, the security application whose protective measures can be foiled to compromise with security, does not guarantee security —Is a biometric device worth investing in? It is very unlikely that the expensive biometric devices are really more secure than the ones tested by us or whether it is simply the case that no one has yet seriously tested them.

Hypothesis 2:

- Null hypothesis (H_0^2): Biometrics security is not complementary to generic security approach.

- Alternative (H_A^2): Biometrics security is complementary to generic security approach.

After all, biometrics weaknesses are well detailed in theory. Before the abolition of passwords or PINs in favour of biometric procedures, our tests have shown that we were able to, with comparatively simple means regardless of high-tech weaponry gain adequate assess to biometric data, replay attack and possession of the database administrator rights under certain conditions. However, as long as adequate security cannot be guaranteed through biometric solutions the use of biometric devices should always be coupled when possible with PINs or passwords. The technology suitable for mass consumption for identifying and authenticating the identity of individuals on the basis of their physical features is obviously still in its infancy!

Outcome of Hypothesis 2

- (H_0^2) is rejected in favour of (H_A^2)

- As a result of the laboratory experiments and all the detailed weaknesses found in the technologies for biometrics, therefore biometrics security is complementary to the generic security approach. The result of the test has proved that as adequate security cannot be guaranteed through biometric solutions, the use of biometric devices should always be coupled when possible with PINs or passwords.

- Apart from the laboratory experiments, all the case studies that were examined shows that biometrics security is complementary to the generic security approach. It is equally important to note that a single biometric identification is not recommended for high security environments.

To determine how vigorously the current biometric security systems are able to resist attempts to compromise. An extensive test on 21 biometrics devices for security loopholes shows that biometrics has high error rate. It should be tested for it ethos and values not to breach the systems rules. Three experiments were conducted to show the validity of current biometrics technologies:

Hypothesis 3:

- Null hypothesis (H_0^3): Absolute security is unattainable on biometrics technologies.

- Alternative (H_A^3): Absolute security is attainable on biometrics technologies.

Experiment 1.

The first experiment relies on tricking the biometrics system with the aid of artificially created data; a precondition for this experiment is to get hold of more or less easily obtainable biometric features of the face and fingerprint. After developing the appropriate photograph(s) and/or creating the artificial fingerprint(s), the copies of features were then implied to attempt obtain authentication. These experiments were performed to test the reliability of the current facial and fingerprint devices.

Result: The outcome of our laboratory experiment based on 21 biometrics devices from different manufacturers failed to detect artificial face and fingerprint. This experiment shows that not all fingerprint devices are built with impulse recognition. Furthermore, the fingerprint test shows that 73 attempts were compromised.

Experiment 2.

The second experiment entails tricking the biometrics system with artificial data by playing back to reference the data sets collected using a USB sniffer program, the biometric sensor is bypassed (a replay attack).

Result: We are able to bypass the biometric sensor using USB sniffer program. The result of our experiment shows that it is possible to extract biometrically relevant data by eavesdropping on the communication via the USB port between the computer and the sensor. It worth noting that USB sniffer program is commonly in use to enable network security to compromise with illegal activities.

Experiment 3.

The third experiment is to attack the database directly and requires possession of the database administrator rights and permission to exchange sets of data used as reference sets for recognition purposes. If data sets have no separate protections of there own the assailant has the opportunity to forge user's data (biometrics profile) with intention to execute the date in a later date.

Result: We are able to attack the biometric database directly and gain possession of the database administrator rights under certain conditions.

Outcome of Hypothesis 3

- (H_A^3) is rejected in favour of (H_0^3)

- As a result of the laboratory experiments and all the detailed weaknesses found in the current biometrics technologies shows that absolute security is unattainable on biometrics. The result of the test has proved that 99.9% of the biometrics devices will require combinatory biometrics profile in order to enhanced generic security.

6.   ALTERNATIVE INTERNATIONAL NETWORKS

The transactions between countries passport/ID card checks, could involve a link between the requesting country and every other country, if each country holds their own separate biometric database. Assuming there are 150 countries this will require each country to have 2250 secure connections. Transactions within countries would not be affected since the national database server replicates the biometrics profile to the international database. However, smaller countries like the Caribbean or the Pacific countries could join together to form a sub-regional biometric collaboration database (see Figure 4–1 for diagrammatic illustration).

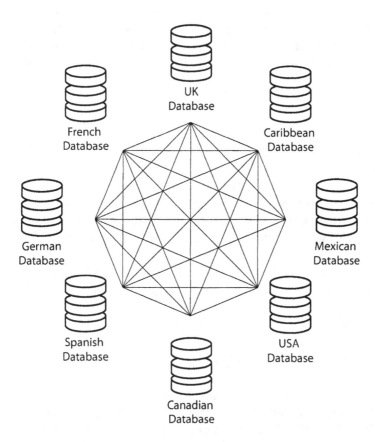

Figure 4–1. Biometrics database connections between countries

The implementation of an international database may raise security concerns about how data will be used and by whom, so it should be strictly controlled and regulated. Under this system each country would need a high security connection with the international database, which would act as a hub to connect with the third party country (see Figure 4–2 for diagrammatic illustration). If the international database is held in Geneva for example and a British citizen is in the USA and requires their identity to be confirmed a request would be made to the UK database via the international centre in Geneva.

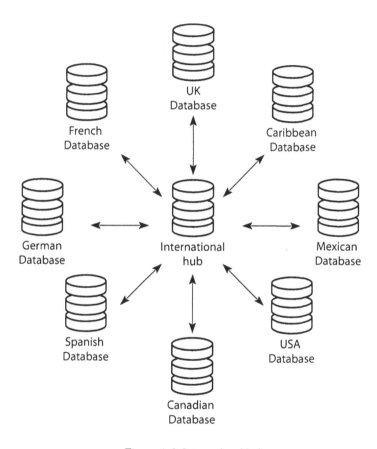

Figure 4–2. International hub

A mid way proposal could involve the use of regional databases connected to an international database. This could be useful since most visits outside a particular country tend to be made to countries within that local region; visits to other regions are less common. For example a British citizen in the USA requiring an identity check, the information would go from the US database to the North American regional database, connecting to the international database then on to the European database and extracts required information from the UK database (see Figure 4-3 for diagrammatic illustration).

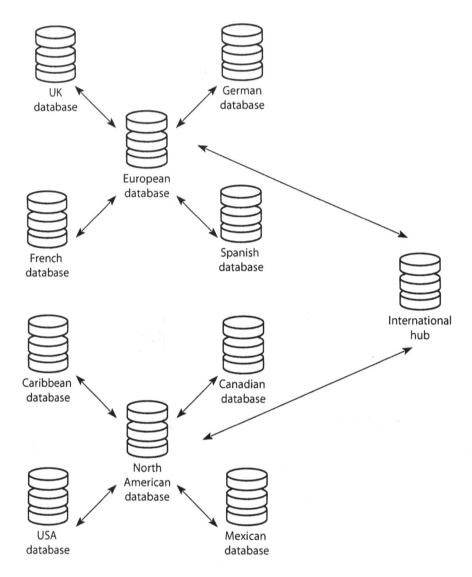

Figure 4–3. International hub

Biometric data in the Europe, USA and many other countries are collated in decentralised databases, so there is an urgent need for the international standards agency to monitor usage of the technology to ensure that it is deployed as efficiently as possible across multiple countries.

7. SHONIREGUN AND CROSIER SECURED BIOMETRICS APPLICATIONS MODEL (SCSBAM)

There has never been a model in existence that specifically addresses how biometric applications should be secured, as a result the Shoniregun and Crosier Secured Biometrics Applications Model (SCSBAM) is proposed. The SCSBAM consists of two phases. Phase 1 is 'Process Combination of Initial Enrolment'. It identifies the 'Initial enrolment using SBAC' 'Routing Transformation', 'Process Composition', 'Verification', 'Identification', 'Enrolment Device', 'Intrinsic Physiological Content', 'Modelling Feature', and 'Database System', while Phase 2 presents the Policy and Monitoring that comprises of 7 key stages: 'Policy', 'Audit', 'Application Adapter', 'Application of all logic' 'Organisation Database', 'National Database', 'International Database', and 'Shared Database System'. The Phases involved in SCSBAM are discusses below. The phases 1 and 2 complement one another; therefore it is not possible to perform a complete process without the interaction of both phases (see Figure 4–4 for diagrammatic illustration).

The large-scale implementation and deployment of biometric systems demand concentration on the security loopholes. The SCSBAM will provide biometric modalities suitable for user identification, verification, and authentication of multiple modalities security. The combination of biometric modalities and the threshold of trust and confidentiality needed for controlled access to the Secured Biometric Application Card (SBAC) are paramount to individuals' privacy. The SBAC contained a chip that stored individual biometric features that can be updated at every point of interaction with the biometrics device for any access clarification. The SBAC has the capacity to store at least three different biometrics features that are previously used by the SBAC holder before validation. To enhance the security of the SBAC we used two-to-three way mapping process.

Phase 1. Process combination of enrolment

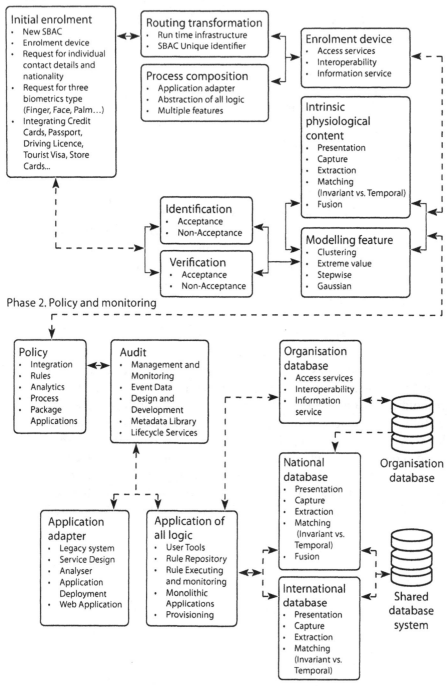

Figure 4–4. Overview of Shoniregun and Crosier secured biometrics applications model
(SCSBAM)

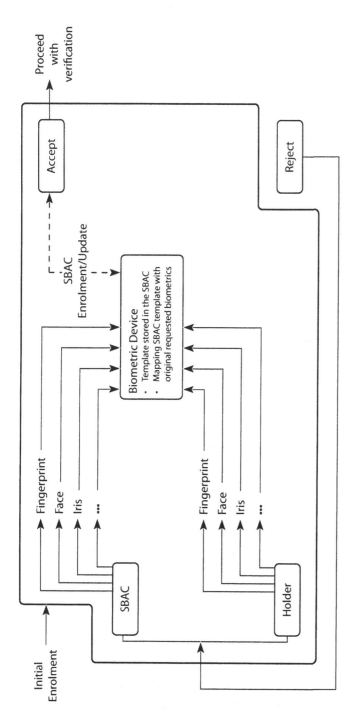

Figure 4–5. SBAC initial enrolment

The SBAC consisted of embedded chip that store biometrics features. The whole process of SBAC starts from the point of contact between an individual and the SBAC, and the first verification starts from the time the SBAC holder inserts the SBAC into the biometric device and a message will appear on the screen asking for a particular biometric from the holder (at least a minimum of three biometric features should be verified before proving the identity of the holder). The verification and identity check should be based on:

- Organisation verification (organisations might be linked to the national database system to enhance security, or governments may require organisations to be linked to the national database system).

- Centralised national database system for protecting national security, the citizens, and for updating international database system.

- International database system can be used for police checks, immigration checkpoints, and collective criminal investigations.

With high security environments, the SBAC requires real time updates and verification from the national database systems. The SBAC will be a joint effort from all participating countries to standardise and regulate policies that can be adhered to.

Phase 1. Process Combination of Enrolment

The 'Initial Enrolment' of SBAC accommodates new and existing holders to enrol and update their biometrics profile at any time without notification. At the enrolment it is expected that some generic questions need to be answered before initiating the process of a new SBAC. The SBAC will be a good platform for integrating credit cards (all credit cards into one easy to carry, with greater choice of what credit card to spend — through one access point), Passport, Driving Licence, Airport check-in, Tourist Visa, Store cards, and household appliances (can be use for turning on/off hi-fi, television, mobile phone, Laptops, and many other devices) and examples of how biometric profiles can enhance electronic government have been cited by Azenabor and Shoniregun (2007).

The 'Routing Transformation', 'Process Composition', and 'Enrolment Device' are tightly coupled to perform the initial enrolment. These jointly perform the validation of the biometrics profile, which are then stored in the

SBAC embedded chip (see Figure 4–5 for diagrammatic illustration). After the SBAC has gone through the 'Initial Enrolment' it has to verify and identify the holder by mapping the template stored in the SBAC chip and the holder's instant biometric profiles with the details provided by 'Intrinsic Physiological Content' and Modelling Feature. The result of the latter will either lead to 'Accept' or 'Reject'. If accepted the process will proceed to the Phase 2, where the matching set generated from the SBAC template and the original biometrics would undergo further system checks. This is the final mapping stage; the biometrics profile is mapped against the previously stored template held on the organisation, or national database system. The national database system automatically updates international database system. It is very important to mention that individual rights of access to the database systems should be significantly minimised and monitored with CCTV 24 hours a day. But on the other hand, if the process reject due to mismatch or any other errors, the SBAC holder will have to go through the process again. But if the SBAC is permanently damaged then the holder will have to go through the whole process starting from the 'Initial Enrolment'.

Phase 2. Policy and Monitoring

The first interaction process in phase 2 involves the policy and auditing that checks the authenticity of individual biometric features. The audit process interfaces the applications adapter and logic. The application adapter converts the data from the application into a common form acceptable for integration with other applications. On the hand the application logic provides an optimal blend of technical consulting and knowledge transfer to structure the biometric profiles. It performs the data entry, update, query and report processing that are based on set of rules. The rules are checked at run time to decide the application's execution path, which provide comprehensive, bi-directional, multimodal, synchronous and asynchronous connectivity between the SBAC and the database systems. Connectivity is available for all supported interface mechanisms. All the processes in phases 1 and 2 take place behind the scenes.

8.   RESULT SUMMARY OF HYPOTHESES

The formal theory, case studies, and laboratory experiments (combinatory research methodology) have been carried out in an attempt to prove or reject the hypotheses stated in chapter 1. The total outcome includes other elements that have led the authors to prove or reject the three hypotheses (see Table

Table 4–2. Summary of hypotheses tested and results

Hypothesis tested	Reason in favour
Hypothesis 1	(H_A^1) Accepted Reason for acceptance of (H_A^1) • Classification and taxonomy of biometrics are attainable • The biometrics technology can work in isolation without generic security approach e.g. PIN Token…(see chapter 2 for further discussion).
Hypothesis 2	(H_A^2) Accepted. Reason for acceptance of (H_A^2) • The biometrics applications can be enabled in some computers and network devices as substitute to typing user's password, therefore biometrics security is complementary to generic security approach. • The biometrics can be synchronised with generic security approach.
Hypothesis 3	(H_0^3) Accepted. Reason for acceptance of (H_0^3) • The limitations of the biometrics technology as led to the poor security performance. • The Internet is a global network with unrestricted boundaries, as a result of this; transactions on the Internet can be intercepted, interrupted, modification, and disinformation or fabrication. • The biometrics systems inherited many of the Internet security problems: i. Security in the application layer cannot be 100 per cent guarantee. ii. The biometrics encryptions require further research. • The results of the questionnaire survey and the laboratory experiments have proved that biometrics devices are not 100 per cent secured and requires further security enhancement. • Security and storage of users biometrics profile is still a major concern.

4–2). The results of the questionnaire survey and the case studies have shown that a staggering number of organisations agreed that absolute security is unattainable on biometrics systems. It is also evident that the biometrics are not complementary to the generic security approach. Previous study has shown that society is exposed to a plethora of security problems (Shoniregun, 2005) and the current biometric systems are not the best security solutions. It is our belief that the adoption of biometric technology would be a way forward to compromise the weaknesses found in the literature review, the questionnaire survey, case studies and laboratory experiments.

9. SUMMARY OF CHAPTER FOUR

Generally speaking, a reliable system can loose its integrity and acceptance and it is a simple fact that password or swipe-card based authentication cannot be relied upon to provide a dependable means of identification. On the other hand, biometrics provide a person with unique characteristics, which are always there. Can they be used as a cryptographic key? Unfortunately, the answer is negative: biometric images or templates are variable by nature (temporal). For example, each new biometric sample is always different (Cavoukian and Stoianov, 2007). Therefore, it is very important to pay attention to how to secure biometric profiles. If biometrics are to become widely adopted and more importantly, widely accepted as a secure identification method, it must be security proven and offer a highly accurate service which cannot be compromised. For a biometric system to have increased security it is necessary to incorporate more than one biometric. If multiple biometrics are to be used then they should be submitted under tightly controlled conditions. However, there are potential problems associated with SBAC, such as:

- Software installation errors

- Software developer errors

- Microchip malfunction

- Data entry error from SBAC holder

- Computer hardware and software failure

- Software package errors

It is clear from the above list that there are many areas in which problems could arise; therefore it is important that all known risks are identified and highlighted, even if some of them are unpopular or unable to compromise to cause any damage and loss of biometrics profiles or denial of services.

REFERENCES

Al mualla, M., 2005. *The UAE iris expellees tracking and Border control system*, http: //www. biometrics.org/bc2005/Presentations/Conference/2%20Tuesday%20September%2020/ Tue_Ballroom%20B/Lt.%20Mohammad%20UAE2005.pdf, (August 29, 2007).

Azenabor, C, E., and Shoniregun, C, A., 2007, 'Electronic Government Security Measures', *Proceedings of the 7th Annual Hawaii International Conference on Business*, May 24-27, 2007, Honolulu, Hawaii. USA.

Benbasat, I., Goldstein, D. K., and Mead, M., 1987, 'The case research strategy in studies of information systems', *MIS Quarterly*, September, pp. 369–386.

Cavoukian, A., and Stoianov, A., (2007), *Biometric Encryption: A Positive-Sum Technology that Achieves Strong Authentication, Security AND Privacy*, http://www.ipc.on.ca/images/ Resources/up-1bio_encryp.pdf, (August 1, 2007).

Galliers, R. D., 1992, 'Information systems planning in the United Kingdom and Australia: a comparison of current practice', *Oxford Surveys in Information Technology*.

Petraborg J., and Scott D., 2006, *Social Welfare Identity Management: Building the Business Case for Public Investment*, http://www.eds.com/industries/government/journal /downloads/ idm_journal_sect6.pdf (July 31, 2007).

Shoniregun, C, A., 2005, *Impacts and Risk Assessment of Technology for Internet Security: Enabled Information Small-Medium Enterprises (TEISMES)*, Springer, New York, USA.

Shoniregun, C. A., 2007, Keynote address: 'Application of Biometrics in Internet Protocol Security', *ECAI 2007*, Pitesti, Romania.

Souza, A., 2006, *Biometrics Accessed*, http://commercecan.ic.gc.ca/scdt/bizmap/interfac e2.nsf/ vDownload/ISA_5540/$file/X_5014595.PDF, (August 1, 2007).

Yin, R., 1994, *Case Study Research, Design and Method*, London: Sage.

Zikmund, 1997, *Business Research Methods*, 5th ed., Sydney: The Dryden Press.

Chapter 5

CRITICAL EVALUATION AND DISCUSSION

1. INTRODUCTION

The public are suspicious about how and where their information would be used, and the real motives of the governments supporting this technology. It has been proposed that police should have access to the national database to verify fingerprints, whereas at the moment they only have access to a database of people who have previously been detained. To help pay for the implementation it has also been proposed that the database be made available for commercial companies such as banks to check the identity of customers, the proposal states that the bank will submit data which will be checked against the national database and a result will only say that the person's identity has or has not been confirmed. The technology also raises problems with reliability and the high number of false accepts and rejects. Under optimal conditions, where users are accustomed to using the equipment the identification rates can be above 90%. In a realistic situation, conditions are unlikely to be optimal and many people will not use the systems regularly enough to be thoroughly competent at using it. The United Kingdoms database will eventually contain the data of 60 million people, which raises a question about how many false positives will be returned and the time it will take to check a submitted biometric with the information held on the database. This chapter critically evaluate the issues relating to this study.

2. THE EUROPEAN COMMISSION'S JOINT RESEARCH CENTRE (JRC)

In April 2005 the IHS commented that the European Commission released a major new study on how biometric technologies will impacts daily European citizens' lives. The report was initiated as a result of the European Union's decision to introduce biometrics in passports, visas and residence permits starting from 2006. This report was compiled by the European Commission's Joint

Research Centre (JRC) at the request of the European Parliament's Committee on Civil Liberties, Justice and Home Affairs. According to the JRC report, biometrics will substantially help in making Europe's borders more secure, facilitating border crossing and enhancing trust in identification documents, thus contributing to the creation of the European area of Justice, Freedom and Security. The development of biometrics technologies will eventually contribute to a secure knowledge-based society, and an approach is needed that brings together different policy areas - security, industrial policy, competitiveness and competition policy - to ensure that Europe reaps the full benefits of government and EU initiatives related to biometric technologies. The report JRC addresses the current lack of data and research by considering the social, legal, economic and technological challenges and analyzing in-depth four biometric technologies—face, fingerprint, iris and DNA. These challenges include:

i.   Economically, the report points out the role EU Member States can play in assisting the emergence of a vibrant European biometrics industry. As the "launch customers" of the first major application of biometrics worldwide, they can push industry towards interoperability and the establishment of common standards that will promote competition and job creation.

ii. Legally, the report concludes that Member States will have to provide the appropriate safeguards for privacy and data protection, thus controlling the use and preventing abuse of biometric data.

iii. Technologically, the report has identified the lack of independent empirical data. Hence, there is an urgent need to conduct large-scale field trials to ensure the successful deployment of biometric systems.

iv. Socially, the report raises the need to focus attention on making biometric applications acceptable to citizens, by clearly setting out their purpose and limitations. At the same time, it cites the risk of creating social exclusion for a small but significant part of the population. This could be because citizens choose not to use the required biometrics or are prevented from doing so by factors such as age or disability. Future systems should endeavour to minimize social exclusion.

The JRC study has identified a number of issues that require further consideration and action so that Europe can benefit from the large-scale deployment of biometric technologies. The use of biometrics can deliver improved convenience and value to individuals. It is expected that once the public becomes accustomed to using biometrics at the borders, their use in commercial applications will follow. The diffusion effect is likely to require the addition of specific provisions on biometrics to the existing legal framework. New legislation will be needed when new applications become widespread and necessary fallback procedures are defined. There is a need to recognise the limitations of biometrics. The above discussion has led to the following recommendations:

i.   The purpose of each biometric application should be clearly defined. The use of biometrics may implicitly challenge the existing trust model between citizen and state since it reduces the scope for privacy and anonymity of citizens. Clarity of purpose is needed to avoid "function creep" and false expectations about what biometrics can achieve. Such clarity is particularly needed to ensure user acceptance.

ii. The use of biometrics to enhance privacy. Biometrics raise fears related to privacy, best expressed by the term "surveillance society," but they also have the potential to enhance privacy as they allow authentication without necessarily revealing a person's identity. In addition, by using multiple biometric features it is possible to maintain related personal information segregated and thus limits the erosion of privacy through the linkage of separate sets of data. The more policy measures are able to encourage the use of biometrics to enhance privacy, the more biometrics will be acceptable to the public at large.

iii. The emergence of a vibrant European biometrics industry. The large-scale introduction of biometric passports in Europe provides Member States with a unique opportunity to ensure that these have a positive impact, and that they enable the creation a vibrant European industry sector. Two conditions would appear to be necessary for this to happen. Firstly, the creation of a demand market based on wide user acceptance, by clearly setting out the purpose and providing appropriate safeguards for privacy and data protection. Secondly, the fostering of a competitive supply market for biometrics. This is unlikely to emerge by itself, so it has to be initiated by governments.

iv. Fallback procedures. Since biometric systems are neither completely accurate nor accessible to all, fallback procedures will be needed. In the case of physical access systems (e.g. border control) skilled human operators need to be available to deal with people that are rightly or wrongly rejected. Whatever the applications, whether in the private or public domain, the fallback procedures should be balanced - neither less secure, nor stigmatized. People with unreadable fingerprints, for example, have the same need for dignity and security as others.

v. Areas for future research. The study has revealed several areas where fur-
    ther data and research is needed. These include:

- *Research and technological development.* Biometric technologies provide a strong mechanism for authentication of identity. Biometrics cannot be lost or stolen, although they can be copied, and they cannot be
  revoked. However, the technology is still under development. Technical
  interoperability and a lack of widely accepted standards, as well as performance and integrity of biometric data are major challenges that need
  to be addressed.

- *Multimodal biometric systems.* Multimodal systems are those, which
  combine more than one biometric identifier. For example, it is planned
  to use face and fingerprints in EU border control systems. Research
  initiatives have been launched on the application of multimodal biometrics in mobile communications (e.g. mobile telephones and other
  devices). However researchers need more test data to work with and
  there is still much work to be done.

- *Large-scale field trials.* So far, empirical data on the real-time, large-
  scale implementation of biometric identification involving a heteroge-
  neous population is limited. Field trials will have to be conducted to
  fill this gap. Such trials could also provide realistic cost-benefit data.
  Moreover, there is a need to exchange best practice and to harmonize
  Member State initiatives. The European Commission's Directorate
  General for Information Society and Media has taken some initiatives
  in this regard.

The main reason for introducing biometric systems is to increase overall
security. However, biometric identification is not perfect - it is never 100%
certain, it is vulnerable to errors and it can be "spoofed." Decision-makers
need to understand the level of security guaranteed through the use of biometric systems and the difference that can exist between the perception and the
reality of the sense of security provided. The biometric system is only one part
of an overall identification or authentication process, and the other parts of that
process will play an equal role in determining its effectiveness.

Being technology-led is a bad idea, but what is the alternative?

—Charles Shoniregun, Keynote speech at ECAI, Romania (2007)

In June 2004, the Conference on Biometrics for the Benefit of the Citizen: a European Perspective was held in Dublin, which detailed the European values, opportunities and the way ahead for biometrics in EU (CEIS, 2004):

i. Europe has key rights and values that are part of our culture, heritage and society and that have to be secured. And, one of these is the right to privacy.

ii. It goes without saying that the use of biometric systems must always be preceded by careful assessment of their potential impact on fundamental rights.

iii. Articles 7 and 8 of the Charter of fundamental rights provide for the right to privacy and for data protection. As regards the latter, specific attention must be given to the fair processing of data, the rule of law and the individual's right to access his or her own data. This implies that important safeguards must be provided, both from both a legal and technical perspective.

iv. At the EU level, Directive 95/46 on data protection provides the framework for gathering and processing of personal data. The principles of this Directive apply to the gathering and processing of biometric data in all biometric systems for authentication and verification purposes. This implies 'inter alia' the respect of certain rights and obligations as well as the independent supervision by competent authorities and, in particular, data protection authorities.

v. In this context, the Commission continues to be committed to consult the Data Protection Commissioners on its relevant legislative proposals.

In the EU, the biometric industry is still rather small but very dynamic as it is mainly made up of very creative and innovative SMEs. Ireland is home to a number of such young and dynamic companies:

i. On the industrial side, the lack of commonly agreed industrial standards and interoperability of biometric systems hinders the possibility for the biometric industry to grow and to benefit from the economy of scale that is slowly developing. This is why the Commission strongly supports interoperability between biometric systems and welcomes and furthers the standardization activity on biometrics carried out at the International level. Once accomplished, this activity will provide industry with the technological framework and guidance that it needs to secure the return of its investments in research and development.

ii. On the research side, the Framework Programme started in the early nineties with seminal projects and progressively developed into significant research activities in FP6 on medium to long term biometric research and on innovative biometric applications like travel documents.

iii. One of the qualifying aspects of the Commission support to R&D for biometrics is to reinforce the EU position in biometric research by favouring and promoting the integration of scientific and technical centres of excellence. In so doing, the Commission supports the realisation of an integrated EU research capability in the biometric area.

The Commission supports the development of non-proprietary, open and interoperable solutions that would help the still young and fragmented EU biometric industry to leverage the economy of scale that would be realised with the coherent approach in our legislative proposals. In the short term, the Commission is promoting a series of initiatives to accompany the rolling out of biometrics in large-scale systems:

i. To promote the establishment of an authoritative industrial and technical structure to support Member States and EU institutions to take informed policy and regulatory decisions on matters pertaining to the deployment of biometrics.

ii. To encourage and support the exchange of information on experience in deployment initiatives in Member States, so as to limit the fragmentation of solutions.

iii. Planning to launch a consultation on how to realise an independent EU Biometrics assessment/certification network that would define commonly agreed "certification" frameworks/protocols to qualify biometrics technologies, products and systems.

iv. Planning to engage the Member States in a discussion on the technical and societal issues in particular, the security and privacy that related to the deployment of biometrics in large-scale security systems. This process shall aim at defining common principles and guidance on how to design, develop and use biometrics in systems for the benefit of the society.

The obligation of States to protect fundamental rights and freedoms of citizens is at the basis of our democratic societies. Biometric applications and systems must therefore be assessed in this perspective. It is very important to strike the appropriate balance between the obligation to guarantee the respect of fundamental rights of individuals and security concerns.

3. TECHNOLOGICAL ENHANCEMENT

The online and offline security concerns have demonstrated that passwords, cards, tokens and single-factor authentication solutions alone cannot adequately address today's growing need to more accurately verify identities to ensure both information and physical security. The following are the current technological enhancement of biometrics devices:

i. The *SecureLink System* provides a solution that's simple to deploy and easy to use. Because it includes not only the biometric authentication device, but also the entire infrastructure organizations need to get the solution up and running very quickly, it overcomes the obstacles that business and government previously faced with biometrics. With this system, there is no longer any need for organizations to put a complex computer infrastructure in place to authenticate and manage the data transmitted by biometric devices because the authentication processing technology is part of the turnkey solution. A wide range of organizations can now add dramatically enhanced identity theft protection to their operations without altering the way in which they do business (Morrison, 2006)

ii. The *FingerChip sensors* already provide a very good fit to Physical Access Control or Point-of-Sale application requirements thanks to their high robustness, low power consumption and high resistance to environmental constraints such as dirt, humidity or extreme temperatures, said David Richard, Atmel's Biometrics Marketing Manager. The AT77C102B improves the image quality output by the sensor. Its full compatibility with its predecessor will make it easy to implement for our current customers while new prospects will appreciate the performance of the sensor. Capitalising on high-performance thermal technology, the AT77C102B FingerChip sensor uses an improved thermal-sensitive layer on top of the silicon. This improvement elevates the maximum temperature that the sensor can withstand, leading to new connection capabilities especially with direct flex report. The AT77C102B is also RoHS-compliant, allowing the complete migration to RoHS for all sensors in the FingerChip product range (Richard, 2006).

iii. The Saflink *SureAccess reader* is the first in a family of products designed to meet the strict requirements of the National Institute of Standards and Technologies' (NIST) Federal Information Processing Standard (FIPS) 201, also known as Personal Identity Verification (PIV) of federal employees and contractors. Designed for interoperability and remote administration, the SureAccess solution easily integrates with many existing physical access control systems and supports the technical specifications of the Transportation Security Administration's (TSA) Transportation Worker Identification Credential (TWIC) program. The SureAccess is based on the same Saflink contactless smart card and biometric reader technology previously deployed by the TSA as part of TWIC Phase III. Rated IP65 for dust and moisture resistance, the system is ideal for outdoor deployments in extreme conditions. SureAccess allows seaports, airports and other critical facilities to deploy a standardized credential that enables workers to use the same smart card to gain entry at multiple sites. The product, also being utilized by the State of Florida in a deepwater seaport security initiative, is designed for broad deployment in public settings for both indoor and outdoor use. The technology has been implemented in TWIC Phase III and the State of Florida deep water port programs. In these deployments, we learned the importance of manufacturing an all-weather biometric device capable of operation in extreme port conditions as well as the need for flexible integration with existing physical access systems to minimize infrastructure cost upgrades (Argenbright, 2006).

iv. The CSC's *IDentity* solution meets the requirements for Homeland Security Presidential Directive 12, which mandates that federal agencies implement robust identification and identity management capabilities. The IDentity is a system of interactive applications based on commercial off-the-shelf products that provide federal agencies with the flexibility they need to implement it in concert with their current technology. This offering will help deliver results to meet the identity management and credentialing needs of our government clients. The IDentity follows the design principles of service-oriented business management architecture. It enables customers to add and remove Web services and new or improved risk and identity assessment analytics at will. This approach makes the system flexible, as well as adaptable in the future. It also includes several features that provide strong identity authentication needed to support federal, state and local homeland security initiatives. Features include: multiple levels of biographic and biometric search capabilities for establishing name uniqueness and integrity; dual multi-modal search fusion engines that enable powerful combinations of biometric algorithms in searches for duplicate or prohibited identities using different matching algorithms; and multi-source, multi-analytic biographic and document data screening capabilities that can incorporate government and public data sources to guard against fraudulent or manufactured identities (Ruggles, 2006).

v. Using an *Infinova* surveillance camera and Fulcrum biometric software, TETRAGATE focuses on providing a solution in which even a laptop, iPod, or other RFID tagged assets can be tied to a human asset to match people who are authorized to be on the property at a given time. Imagine hundreds of people passing through a 'portal' with powerful long-range, unobtrusive cameras capturing facial images that are matched against a data archive at a rate of 60,000 images per second, the secondary identification is made as individuals' RFID credentials are read and matched to biometric records. Any exception to the match-ups triggers a security situation, based on business rules in place, focusing on the specific individuals, while others continue on uninterrupted (Stryczek, 2006). All human or physical assets can be linked into and managed by a single, formidable database that provides effective and total flexibility of configuration and integration. Global standards for data synchronisation, automatic identification, biometric technology and RFID ensure that TETRAGATE will scale to meet the specific needs of any organization. Development of the system began after the events of September 11, 2001, when an insurer emphasized the critical importance of knowing who the people are onsite at a particular location and time. What might seem like an uncomplicated task under normal circumstances had its problems. For example, employees and contractors politely holding a door open as other people pass through might not know if one or more of those "others" has the proper ID card or authorization. The best methods of identifying people are retina scanning, fingerprinting, and face mapping, clearly these methods not usually possible with large groups of people moving through entryways at once.

vi. Our society is becoming increasingly more dependent on mobility, which increases the need for access to wireless networks to conduct business, biometrics division. The *Bio-NetGuard* takes the concern out of controlling a WiFi local area network by fully containing it through a biometric authentication device that works with any access point. The WiFi networks provide a tremendous solution to the demands of an increasing mobile workforce, but there are still concerns about verifying who can and cannot access the network. There have been ways to protect WiFi-enhanced equipment in the past, but no methods to authenticate those who connect to the wireless system. The Bio-NetGuard allows an IT Manager to secure the network against unauthorized users by requiring biometric fingerprint authentication prior to gaining access to the network, either through their desktop or personal computers, laptops or PDAs. The Bio-NetGuard uses a Fujitsu MBF200 sensor and is 802.11a/b/g and 802.11i compliant based on DSP, fully contained network authentication device that works with any WPA-compliant access point. It enabled organisations and companies, to secure their wireless devices and increase security of confidential information and files. It is a plug-and-play device and requires no more than a few minutes to install and configure. It supports up to 500 users and has a fingerprint match time of 400 milliseconds. This works with a large number of WiFi access points including Netgear WG102, Linksys WAP54G, Cisco AIR-ONET 1100, D-Link DWL-7100AP, and a number of WiFi adapter cards and chipsets including INTEL Centrino, Netgear 11T, Linksys WPC11, Cisco AIRONET 350, and D-Link DWL-G650 (Bradt, 2006).

vii. The *Panasonic Iris Readers* deliver fast and accurate system enrollment and authentication without the need for any physical contact, No other non-invasive identification system is as precise, easy to use or as enduring as Panasonic's Iris Readers. The new BM-ET200 Iris Reader is simple to configure and provides recognition results in only 0.3 seconds. A dual mirror configuration makes it easy for the individual to align the eyes for accurate reading, capturing a detailed image of both irises for maximum accuracy. Voice instructions guide the user's position for optimal performance. The BM-ET200 can either be used as part of a stand-alone system or integrated into a larger network. The Iris recognition technology allows fast one-to-many searches on an extremely large database. The system's enrollment and authentication algorithm, developed by Iridian Technologies, Inc., makes a template or "map" of each person's iris pattern, for storage on a database or onto an access card or token. To verify identity, an individual simply 'looks into' a Panasonic Iris Reader and the system compares his/her iris pattern images with iris templates stored in the database or portable device. If there is a match, the identity is verified (DeFina, 2006).

viii. The *Mobio*'s proprietary technology combines the power of cryptography and security of portable biometrics to enable a high-security identity system for voice verification, information sharing and network and physical access control. This technology is one universal ID designed to access all points in an organization creating simplicity, efficiency and security. What makes the Cryptolex system unique is its backend server-to-server integration that enables Mobio to be used concurrently for building/door access, network login, VPN, and web applications. While Mobio looks similar to an authentication token or fingerprint reader, it is based on a newly developed technology that leverages cryptography to create a strong backend trust solution that can be utilized within an organization or across legally separate entities. Identity verification is one of the biggest challenges facing organizations of all types as we increasingly rely on digital systems for everything from everyday transactions to military applications. While we know that password security is weak, many obstacles exist to widespread adoption of stronger authentication methods, ranging from privacy concerns for users to integration challenges for organizations. Using Mobio, an organisation can have an employee use one device to prove their identity when accessing a building, joining a sensitive teleconference, and logging into their corporate email account or to demonstrate their authorization to download sensitive files from the corporate server. Its flexibility comes from its unique design, which leverages biometrics and cryptography to convert individual fingerprints into dynamic numbers, called Biocodes. Mobio Biocodes are completely random numbers that never repeat, are only valid for a few seconds and are legally binding digital signatures that can be logged, tracked and audited. The Biocodes are designed and distributed in such a manner that replay and man-in-the-middle attacks are effectively eliminated. Unlike traditional biometric-based solutions, Mobio is completely portable, does not require central storage of biometric information and Biocodes can be used anywhere a password is required, even if no network connection is available. There is no threat of identity theft or fraud if Mobio is lost or stolen, as it cannot be unlocked or misused by an unauthorized user and will only generate a Biocode based on the owner's specific fingerprint. Mobio is the flagship product behind Cryptolex's Universal ID System (UID™), a flexible combination of hardware and software components that power a number of identify verification applications, which include: voice Control, document Control, network Access Control, and physical Access Control (Najm, 2006).

ix. The revolutionary *SmartScan technology* completely eliminates the need for a key or key code, utilizing only a fingerprint scan. The Kwikset's SmartScan is a biometrically accessible deadbolt door lock system that can be applied to internal and external doors in residential applications based on power bolt mechanism. Simply swiping a valid fingerprint across its sensor activates the SmartScan deadbolt. This technology reads sub dermal fingerprint patterns located beneath the outer surface layer of the skin, making it unaffected by dirty or worn fingertips. Programmable with up to 50+ user fingerprints, it also has a special timed "lock out feature" that allows homeowners three levels of access options. This feature allows continual access (24/7) for family members, temporary access for house sitters or contractors, and time restricted access for babysitters or housekeepers. However, consumer acceptance of SmartScan technology is accelerating. It is currently available on portable hard drives and IBM ThinkPad computers, as well as in grocery store checkouts, gas stations and automobiles. Biometrics is an emerging technology that can give consumers an increased level of home protection and peace of mind. It can be easily installed on most standard doors and requires no hard wiring. The durable, low power consumption system operates on a battery with a life of one year (based on 20 accesses per day) (Lundquist, 2007).

x. The first product released is BioLink IDenium for Active Directory (AD), the only biometric solution for Active Directory supporting the 1-to-many identification mode, i.e. not requiring any other parameters for quick identification. Designed for Windows NT/2000/XP, it allows users registered in one domain getting biometrically identified with their unique fingerprints while accessing the shared network resources in the other domain. The offering is characterized by all the key benefits of the entire product line, such as reliability, security, functionality, performance, efficiency, economic feasibility and ease of installation and maintenance. The implementation of BioLink IDenium for AD provides the following advantages: reliable identity verification in multiple domains, secured access to shared PCs, as well as robustness and scalability. BioLink IDenium for AD is also beneficial for reducing the user administration burden thanks to self-enrolment of biometric identifiers by IDenium users, and for its detailed manuals covering all the aspects of its installation and usage in every detail. The product is bundled with BioLink's fingerprint matching devices - U-Match Match-Books v.3.5 -demonstrating high quality capturing of fingerprint images, fast and accurate fingerprint matching. In addition, BioLink IDenium for AD supports a number of biometric scanners from other leading biometric vendors. The core of the system is the biometric server storing the fingerprint database and performing the biometric matching procedures. The key utility of BioLink IDenium for AD provides biometric identification by a fingerprint when logging on the operating system. Another component allows replacing passwords with fingerprint identification while accessing the protected files and applications. The synchronization agent is responsible for synchronizing data between the AD service and BioLink IDenium for AD. At last, the admin pack is designed to enrol new users and their fingerprints centrally on the administrator workstation. Users can enrol their fingerprints, all ten of them, themselves; which is of vital importance if the user cuts or otherwise damages a finger - then he/she can apply another finger and be successfully identified into the system. This long-awaited offering, intuitive in operation, is turning over a new leaf in BioLink's software product line. Taking full advantage of the enterprise-class directory services and management capabilities of the Active Directory enables the users of BioLink IDenium for AD to considerably extend the use of biometrics on their desktops, which will become their second nature. In addition, the product can be regarded as an integral part of the integrated corporate security system, also encompassing BioLink's physical access control and time management components (Pertsov, 2007).

xi. The Fidelica's platform is the first in the industry that allows fingerprint imaging, enrolment, and authentication to be contained entirely within a standard credit card-sized package. Utilizing the BCP-3, integrators can create a smart card with a radically advanced feature set that works with existing card readers, wireless systems, and other card infrastructure. Biometric security can be added to a system simply by upgrading cards. The beta BCP platform has already been implemented in several different configurations, including the DIVAcard biometric ID for URU Technologies, Inc. The DIVAcard will be used for federal government infrastructure security at sensitive sites such as airports and harbours. We needed a biometric authentication system that ensures conclusive user ID while protecting user privacy, Fidelica has created an embedded system that allowed biometric identification to the identity credential, bringing security up to today's requirements, while protecting the customer's existing investments. The Fidelica offers a unique biometric platform for smart cards, based on its proprietary fingerprint imaging and authentication technology. The company's fingerprint sensor, constructed of thin, flexible, polymer materials, is compact and robust, making it ideal for embedded applications. In the BCP-3 platform, the sensor is coupled with an efficient minutia-based fingerprint matching algorithm and advanced embedded electronics. This combination results in a system that meets industry standards for performance and government and international standards for content and format. The BCP-3 platform will allow developers to achieve a balance in privacy and security that has long been sought after. With the entire system on the card, all processes using personal data (fingerprint acquisition, image processing, fingerprint storage and matching) take place on the card. The cardholder's biometric data is held exclusively on the card; no data leaves the card except a match/no match decision (Conforti, 2007).

xii. The UR Secured® Biometric Fingerprint Encryption Mouse (BioM-SL300) provides users with convenient log in to Windows® with the single swipe of a finger, establish a password bank for storing login information for registered web sites, lock and unlock the system, and protect access to files/folders on the computer's hard drive. It also creates the virtual disk on the computer's hard drive, registered user and fingerprint verification. The built in fingerprint reader allows authorized users access to the encrypted data on the computer with the swipe of a finger. Once the print is confirmed, the user is allowed access to their confidential information. Since an individual fingerprint or thumbprint is the password, the password to your secure drive can never be stolen, forged, or forgotten (B & J Biometrics, 2006).

However, the strong authentication systems have posed interoperability and manageability challenges for organisations, users and have led to the slow widespread adoption of biometrics.

4.   ETHICAL IMPLICATIONS

There are serious ethical implications for holding biometric data by central governments and other agencies. Concerns about identity theft and biometrics have still to be resolved. If their credit card details are stolen it can cause problems, but if their iris scan is stolen, this may allows access to personal information or financial services, the damage could be irreversible. Biometric technologies have often been rolled out without adequate safeguards for personal information that has been collected on behalf of individuals. Biometrics have been put forward as a way of reducing criminality, but it is just as likely that they could be used to reduce the personal liberties of law abiding citizens. Developments made in digital video, x-ray, wireless technology, global positioning satellite systems, biometrics, image scanning, voice recognition and DNA, provide governments with new ways to 'search' individuals and collect vast amounts of information on innocent law abiding members of the public. As technology improves and its use increases, more private companies and public utilities will use biometrics for safe accurate identification. These advances also raise concerns among society. First, the physical effects of using the technology, can it cause physical harm to the user, e.g. are retinal scanners clean and hygienic to use. Secondly, can personal information be misused, tampered with or sold, e.g. criminals could steal or copy biometric data, which may then be used in unauthorised ways without the consent of the individual.

The introduction of facial recognition, in conjunction with video surveillance could become more intrusive. Once the technology is installed, it is unlikely to remain confined to the original objective, which could have implications for personal freedoms. Video monitoring is also regarded as an intrusive form of surveillance, which can be used to record in graphic detail, personal and private behaviour. There is also the possibility that video monitoring could be misused. The UK has one of the highest concentrations of CCTV in public areas, but camera operators have been shown to focus disproportionately on coloured people, and the mainly male operators focus voyeuristically on women. Facial recognition can also be open to abuse, since it does not require the consent of the person being identified. A line has to be drawn between the infringement on person freedoms and the reduction in crime that occurs in areas where CCTV is installed. When implemented correctly, biometrics can provide an absolute certainty that you cannot be impersonated, and you also retain your privacy. It is not biometrics, which is seen as an invasion of privacy, it is the implementation and storage of the related biometric data. Databases can be used to link personal information from disparate sources without user consent and are the source of much of the privacy world's concern about information aggregation and misuse. The biggest danger occurs when the biometrics are used to find out about what an individual does, rather that just who they are. Existing links between databases are used to investigate people's behaviour, such as combining medical, social security and financial data, with the advent of biometrics it has focused peoples minds onto the consequences of government being able to track everyone's every action. The problem of databases sharing information, legally or illegally, can be prevented by keeping biometric templates in a secure token such as a smart card, with storage and portability of data. Using read only tokens such as smart cards, makes it much more difficult for an adversary to gain access to the biometric template. The card or token could also be protected using its own secret encryption and signing keys, adding another level of security to the identification process, as well as strongly protecting every card holder's privacy. The technology used to record biometric data is not 100 per cent secure. There are also high levels of concern about privacy and the security of the information. If biometrics are to become widely accepted then these pre-conceptions must be overcome, and real measures must be taken to maintain the confidentiality of the information being held. Biometrics does raise three main privacy concerns (Prabhakar et al., 2003):

i. *Unintended functional scope.* Since biometric identifiers are biological in origin; collectors may ascertain additional personal information from scanned biometric measurements. For instance, certain malformed fingers may be correlated with certain genetic disorders. With the rapid advances in genome research there may be an increased fear of inferring further information from biological measurements. Such use of biometric information may lead to systematic discrimination against segments of the population regarded as 'risky'.

ii. *Unintended application scope.* Strong biometric identifiers such as fingerprints allow the possibility of unwanted identification. For instance persons
legally maintaining aliases for safety reasons could be identified based on
their fingerprints. Also biometric identifiers could link bits and pieces of
behavioural information about individuals enrolled in widely different applications. Detractors often construe this potential as a means for organisation, government or corporate, to accumulate power over individuals and
their autonomy.

iii. *Covert recognition.* Biometrics is not secret. It is often possible to obtain
a biometric sample, such as a person's face without their consent. This
permits covert recognition of previously enrolled individuals. Thus those
who wish to remain anonymous in a particular situation would have their
privacy denied by biometrics. These possible abuses of biometric information and related accountability procedures can be addressed in a number of
ways:

- Legislation by governments, e.g., the European Union legislation
against sharing biometric identifiers and personal information.

- Assurance of self-regulation, e.g., a consortium of biometric vendors
could choose to adhere to a set of ethical guidelines in their product
design.

- Autonomous enforcement by independent regulatory organisations,
such as a central biometric authority.

Generally speaking, many people will be unwilling to provide biometric data
to centralised applications, or for untrustworthy applications. At present the
most acceptable system will be the highly decentralised applications using encrypted databases over which the public has complete control. A system could
for example issue a smart card containing a fingerprint template, which could
be used to match a fingerprint given on a reader. Most commercial fingerprint
readers do not store the fingerprints. The machine takes a digital photograph,
from which unique features are extracted, which is then turned into a mathematical template, which is then stored. The template takes up less storage
space and it is virtually impossible to recreate a replica of the original fingerprint from the template since it does not contain enough data. Companies
in the USA who routinely screen new recruits for criminal records send the
fingerprints to the FBI, but the FBI has issued assurances that it does not store
these fingerprints once they have been checked (Roberts, 2003). There is often

confusion about identification and verification. Identification establishes exactly who someone is, which involves an actual investigation into a person's true identity, currently this is restricted to criminal and immigration investigations. Verification is not as far reaching as identification since we remain unsure who is who, until they say who they are. European privacy legislation has put strict requirements on the ways in which biometrics can be used. Grijpink (2001) suggests the following rules must be followed:

- *Sectoral boundaries.* Information from one sector cannot be automatically exchanged with another sector, e.g., healthcare cannot share patient information with financial institutions.

- *Clear, recognisable and permissible objective.* The use of biometrics must be clearly stated and everyone should be aware that biometric information is being collected.

- *Proportionality.* The use of biometrics should be in proportion to the level of security, which is required.

- *Subsidiary.* Meaning not having to take things to a higher authority. The systems should be operated at a sectoral level, and should avoid becoming too centralised.

- *Precise delineation of the target group.* The target group should be specified and approach terms and conditions lay down in a contract or by legislation.

- *Security.* A breach of the data only becomes an offence if the biometric data is protected against alteration or access. Therefore the system should be made secure.

- *External supervision.* It may be desirable to have the biometric data supervised by an independent body. This would increase the confidence, which consumers have in biometrics.

Inevitably there will need to be a degree of trading off between security provided by the use of biometrics and the increased loss of privacy. If it is done sensitively with the cooperation of all users, who are given confidence that data collected is securely stored, and cannot be altered or stolen by a third party, biometrics is likely to become accepted. Without a high level of confidence, biometric systems will not become accepted. If they are imposed on members of the public by a higher body, either government or private, they will produce high levels of public resentment and mistrust about the way in which the information, which is collected, is used.

5.   IMPACTS OF BIOMETRICS ON WORLD GOVERNMENTS

Various governments around the world are either employing or considering deploying biometric-based systems for identification and verification purposes. Acharya, (2006) conducted a survey of major programs in use or under development by the US, Canada, and the European Union. The programs are discussed below.

5.1   United States

The United States government is a world leader in the introduction of biometric-based technologies for verification and identification purposes. It has several programs and systems in use or planned that employ biometrics, and some of the major ones are described below:

i.   *Integrated Automated Fingerprint Identification System (IAFIS).* The U.S. Department of Justice's FBI maintains the IAFIS; an automated 10-fingerprint matching system that captures rolled prints. The IAFIS became operational in 1999 and, with fingerprints for more than 47 million subjects on file; it is the largest biometric database in the world.

ii. *United States Visitors and Immigrant Status Indicator Technology (US-VISIT) Program.* The US-VISIT program, established by the Department of Homeland Security (DHS) and launched in 2004, collects, maintains, and shares information, including biometric identifiers, on selected foreign nationals entering and exiting the United States. US-VISIT uses digital finger scans and photographs to screen persons against watch lists (of criminals, terrorists and immigration violators), and to verify that a visitor is the person who was issued a visa or other travel document. Visitors also confirm their departure by having their visas or passports scanned and by undergoing finger scanning at selected air and sea ports of entry. Biometric data are stored in the Automated Biometric Identification System (IDENT) database, and include fingerprint information from the FBI's IAFIS. Full integration between IDENT and IAFIS is a goal. The program has come under attack from the U.S. Government Accountability Office (GAO), which says that the DHS has been very slow in assessing and testing basic system security and privacy controls. The GAO also noted that the DHS had not demonstrated that the program is producing or will produce "mission value commensurate with expected costs and risks." In particular, the department's return-on-investment analyses for exit processes were singled out as not demonstrating that these exit procedures will be cost-effective (United States Government Accountability Office, 2006).

iii. *Registered Traveler (RT) Program.* The RT Program is under development by the DHS. The program will be a voluntary, fee-based, market-driven initiative offered by the private sector with government oversight. The program's goal is to 'strengthen aviation security and enhance customer service'. Companies that enrol participants in the program will collect fingerprints, iris biometrics, and basic biographic information from applicants (frequent flyers). Information collected will then be analysed by the DHS to conduct 'threat screening' in advance of travel for individuals participating in the program. Individuals who participate in the program will, in theory, be provided with expedited screening at the airport. Government-operated pilot programs for RT ran in five US airports in 2004 and 2005, and an evaluation of these pilots deemed the program to be "viable". A public-private partnership pilot was also conducted at the airport in Orlando, Florida. A national rollout of the RT program was originally scheduled for June 2006, but the Web site of the Transport Security Administration (TSA) states that implementation will begin later in 2006 (United States Department of Homeland Security, 2005). Various groups are opposed to the RT program. The Air Transport Association of America states that 'the program will unnecessarily drain limited TSA resources and detract from the agency's ability to craft more comprehensive programs benefiting all travellers'. The American Civil Liberties Union suggests that the initiative would force Americans to choose between preserving their most private and personal information and speeding through airport security. Furthermore, the group argues that the program could make the United States more vulnerable to terrorist attacks since terrorists could enrol in the program by using fake identification (Sparapani, 2006).

5.2   Canada

The Canadian federal government, either alone or in collaboration with the U.S. federal government, employs biometric-based technologies in several programs. It is likely that the use of these technologies will increase, especially in light of changes to international passport standards and proposed changes to passport requirements for travel to the United States. A description of the major federal programs, departments or agencies that employ, or plan to use, biometric technologies are provided below.

i. *Royal Canadian Mounted Police (RCMP).* The RCMP recently began upgrading its fingerprint identification system to improve its speed and accuracy. The new Automated Fingerprint Identification System (AFIS) will support the accurate processing of good-quality fingerprint submissions with little or no manual intervention. The transfer of 4 million fingerprint files from the old AFIS to the new AFIS was projected to be completed in the summer of 2006. A new server will permit the electronic exchange of fingerprint identification requests. The new systems should be in operation by the end of 2006 (RCMP, 2006).

ii. *CANPASS Air.* CANPASS Air is a Canada Border Services Agency (CBSA) program that is intended to facilitate "efficient and secure entry into Canada for pre-approved, low-risk air travellers." The program, which is currently available at seven Canadian airports, uses iris recognition technology to verify a passenger's identity. Under the program, citizens and permanent residents of Canada who wish to participate in the program undergo security checks at registration and every year upon renewal. For an annual fee (currently $50), members of the program receive an identification card that enables them to use the self-serve CANPASS Air kiosks at airports where their iris is photographed and the image compared to that stored in the database. Once their identity is confirmed, individuals then proceed to baggage claim and leave the customs premises without further interaction with a CBSA officer unless they are selected randomly for inspection.

iii. *NEXUS.* The NEXUS is a group of fee-based programs operated jointly by the Canadian and U.S. federal governments that arose from the Canada-United States 30-point Action Plan of the Smart Border Declaration signed in December 2001. For the three NEXUS programs – NEXUS Highway, NEXUS Marine and NEXUS Air – biometrics (fingerprints) are taken as part of the application process to perform a background check. Once approved by both Canada and the United States as low-risk travellers, NEXUS members benefit from a simplified entry process when travelling across the Canada-United States border by motor vehicle, recreational boat or aircraft.

The NEXUS Air is a pilot program that began in November 2004 and operates only at the Vancouver International Airport. It offers expedited customs and immigration clearance to pre-approved, low-risk passengers travelling between Canada and the United States. The program works in a similar fashion to CANPASS Air by employing iris recognition technology to verify a passenger's identity. Once an individual's identity has been confirmed by one of the automated kiosks located in the airport, members answer either U.S. or Canadian (depending on their destination) customs and immigration questions using a touch screen at the kiosk. The kiosk then issues a receipt and members entering Canada are directed towards either the exit or the secondary inspection area. Members flying to the United States are directed to either the secondary inspection area or on to security screening.

iv. *Passport Canada.* The enhancement of security features has been added to Canadian passports issued domestically since 2002 and from April 2006 for Canadian passports issued abroad. These features include a digital photo, holograms, special ink and a machine-readable zone at the bottom of the personal information page. Canadian passports do not currently contain biometric identifiers, but biometrics will likely be included in the newest version of the Canadian passport that is in development. In September 2004, amendments to the Canadian Passport Order were brought into force, two of which allow Passport Canada to include biometrics in passports. The first amendment provides Passport Canada with the authority to convert any information submitted by an applicant into a digital biometric format for the purpose of inserting that information into a passport. The second amendment authorizes Passport Canada to convert an applicant's photograph into a biometric template for the purpose of verifying the applicant's identity.

Passport Canada is currently developing its new 'e-passport' The document will meet ICAO standards, which call for the inclusion of an electronic contact less chip containing, among other items, a digital photo for facial recognition purposes. The agency has released little information publicly about the e-passport project. According to its Corporate and Business Plan 2005-2008, e-passport specimens were to be tested with Canadian diplomats and ministers as part of a pilot project in July 2006, and a national rollout of the documents would happen in July 2007. The agency now says, however, that 'the e-passport is at a developmental stage, and it is premature to discuss cost as well as timeframe for the launch of the e-passport project' (Acharya, 2006). At present, Passport Canada is moving ahead with a separate (and it claims unrelated) project to introduce a facial recognition system to be used during the application process. The system would, when fully operational, perform identification and verification tasks, and would compare applicants' facial images to those on a watch list compiled from a variety of sources. The system would assist Passport Canada "in making and supporting entitlement and passport issuance decisions." The introduction of facial recognition technologies and biometric passports is being done with little or no public debate. Some critics of the process to introduce an e-passport suggest that the federal government is engaging in "policy laundering" – introducing policies developed by foreign and international forum (in this case the issuance of biometric passports that meet ICAO standards) that might not otherwise win approval through the regular domestic political process (Clement and Boa, 2006)

Passport Canada has submitted a Privacy Impact Assessment on the e-passport initiative to the Office of the Privacy Commissioner. The office is not opposed to the inclusion of biometric identifiers per se in passports, but does have some concerns that it says the Passport Office should address about the security of the information included on the proposed e-passport's chip. The Office has indicated that any e-passport system should protect passport holders against such activities as "skimming" and "eavesdropping." Skimming refers to the process whereby someone uses an unauthorized reader to collect the information in a passport's chip surreptitiously, such as when the passport is in someone's pocket. Eavesdropping involves someone intercepting and reading the transmission between the passport's chip and the reader (Office of the Privacy Commissioner of Canada, 2006).

5.3   European Union (EU)

In 2004, the European Commission issued a regulation (that is binding for all Member States except the United Kingdom and Ireland (26) that sets out minimum-security standards for passports and travel documents (Council Regulation (EC), 2004) The regulation stipulates that passports and travel documents shall include a storage medium, which shall contain a facial image, and that the documents shall also include two fingerprints in interoperable (across the EU) formats. All Member States had until 28 August 2006 to implement the facial image requirement, and have until 28 June 2009 to implement the fingerprint requirement. Critics of the EU's planned biometric passports scheme note that the inclusion of a digitised photograph in passports meets the standards set by the ICAO, but that the EU has gone further by requiring the inclusion of fingerprints. They also point out that since only two fingerprints will be taken, the error rate for an EU-wide database will be relatively high if it is to be used for identification (rather than just verification) purposes (Statewatch News editorial, 2006). The EU has decided that the standard

EU passport should contain both fingerprints and an electronic facial image. This will also be extended to those requesting visas and to refugees. Research into the devices for fingerprint recording has shown that the current standard resolution of 500 pixels per inch (ppi) offers insufficient resolution and it has been decided that the standard should be set at 1000 ppi. In response to this the manufacturers of AFIS have adapted their systems to include this higher resolution requirement. The disadvantage of a 1000 ppi resolution is that it requires 4 times the storage capacity. Liveness detection is a problem with all biometrics. A fingerprint can be quite easily faked, using ready available items such as glue. To combat fraud most fingerprint scanners are supervised by a person who ensures that fraud does not take place. A non-supervisory system would be desirable, such as the 'Lumidigm' system operated at Disneyworld to prevent people passing tickets to others after they have finished visiting the park. On the first entry to the park a fingerprint is taken as a match for that ticket, the readers also detect liveness; they do this quickly and process 200,000 people a day. The technology is based on multi-spectral optical technology, which can even capture fingerprints from fingerprints, which are worn, wet, very dry or very dirty. Liveness detection in fingerprints can also be carried out using vein pattern technology which measures the blood vessels within finger and can even detect blood flow. The amount spent on biometrics in the EU was 7.3 million Euros in 2000, by 2006 it had reached 212 million euros, but by 2010 it is forecast to rise to 614.9 million Euros. This increase is largely down to the implementation of biometrics to passports and identity cards. The current state of development of biometric identity documents varies across Europe. The summaries of each countries current state of development are as follows:

i.   *Austria.* The citizen's card or Burgerkarte is a fully operational electronic ID card. Concerns have been raised about the use of RFID in electronic passports.

ii.   *Belgium.* The Belgian Personal Identity Card was announced in 2003 as a fully electronic ID card. It is the size of a credit card and allows easier access to government services. New passports will include a contactless microchip to store personal information and biometric identifiers. The preferred biometric is facial but with the option of fingerprints as a second biometric identifier.

iii. *Cyprus.* So far legislation is being passed to allow the introduction of biometric ID cards and passports.

iv.   *Czech Republic.* E-passports introduced in 2006, estimated that 200,000
        would be issued by end of 2006, with estimates of about 500,000 a year
        after that.

v.   *Germany.* New electronic passport, known as the e-pass has been re-
        leased in Germany. It incorporates a RFID chip to store personal infor-
        mation and the biometric data. In early 2007 the existing facial biomet-
        ric will be joined by a scan of the left and right index fingers, a third
        biometric could be added at a later date. In embassies in the Philippines
        and Nigeria the biometrics in the form of a digital photograph of visa
        applicants have been sent back to Germany to be checked. In February
        2006 it was revealed that the new passport was vulnerable to attack. The
        government of the Federal Republic of Germany continues to consider
        biometric procedures important tools in the fields of identity ascertain-
        ment and criminal prosecution. This emerges from the answer given
        on April 24th to the official question posed to the government by the
        speaker on domestic policy of the parliamentary group of the PDS (the
        Party of Democratic Socialists, Germany's reformed ex-communists),
        Ms. Ursula Jelpke. Making reference to the error rates of biometrics rec-
        ognition systems and the current state of affairs with regard to the pos-
        sible introduction of biometric data to identity cards and the response to
        the official question, the German ministry of interior declared that no
        bill on the introduction of biometric features and storage of the identity
        documents would be introduced to the parliament until the requisite
        preliminary work had been completed. As a first step the procedures in
        question would have to be tested 'in pilot projects of considerable scope
        that as to their environmental features simulate as closely as possible
        the actual later environment of use of the applications.' According to
        the ministry, there is thus no fixed date for the introduction of the bill.
        The use of biometric procedures with regard to identity documents had,
        however, already been discussed at a ministerial level within the EU,
        the ministry's statement continued, and for June 2002 a conference on
        this topic of all EU member states was planned. As there are presently
        at least five totally different biometrics approaches vying for the cus-
        tomers' favour and the scale of a later application at a total of 70 million
        owners of German ID documents is clearly defined, the testing is likely,
        from a technical point of view at least, to take up some time yet.

vi.   *Denmark.* Contract was given to a private company 'Setec' in 2004 to
        provide 3 million biometric passports over the next 5 years. The pass-
        ports will be produced in Finland.

vii.   *Estonia.* One of the first countries in the EU to issue a fully electronic ID card, and biometric passports are in development.

viii.   *Spain.* Progress has not been as fast in Spain compared to other EU states. Electronic ID cards are being introduced, containing an electronic chip containing a digitised photograph, fingerprint and a digital signature. ID card was officially launched by the Spanish Police Department in March 2006, a year later than expected.

ix.   *Finland.* E-passports were introduced in May 2005, at an estimated rate of 400,000 per year. These passports contain high security features, including a polycarbonate data page containing a 'contact less' crypto processor chip storing the holders personal details and biometric identifiers. Fingerprints will be added to the original facial data in 2006-7.Extra security features above those required by the ICAO are also planned, they include; a personal identity code, prevention of unauthorised reading, copying or substitution of the chip and encryption of data communication between chips and chip readers.

x.   *France.* There has been opposition in France to the way in which the ID card is being introduced. The project aims to build a national centralised police database containing the biometric data and the address of each citizen. Concern has been raised about the possiblity of personal data being read from the microchip without the knowledge of the cardholder. Personal information for the ID card and the new e-passports will be held on a central database, while the biometric data will be held anonymously in separate files. The smart chip will be bi-modal, with contact for authentication and contact less for identity information. Issuing of the cards has been delayed and is now not expected until 2008.

xi.   *Greece.* The Hellenic Data Protection Authority announced on 10th November 2003 that collecting biometric data would breach Greek data privacy laws. Despite this e-passports were introduced in June 2006.

xii.   *Hungary.* Progress has been slow, new laws needed to be passed to allow further developments to be put in place.

xiii.   *Ireland.* Due to the high number of visits to the USA by Irish citizens the Irish government decided to implement biometric passports, to maintain visa waiver travel to the USA.

xiv.   *Italy.* Over 13 million smart cards have been issued, but no date has yet been set for the introduction of biometric passports.

xv.   *Lithuania.* The infrastructure for the development of e-passports is still under development.

xvi.   *Luxembourg.* The infrastructure for the development of e-passports is still under development.

xvii. *Latvia.* The infrastructure for the development of e-passports is still under development.

xviii. *Malta.* The infrastructure for the development of e-passports is still under development.

xix.   *Netherlands.* Biometric passports were introduced in mid 2006. A new passport issuing system has also been installed to offer enhanced quality. It has also been discovered that biometric documents are less robust that traditional passports.

xx.   *Poland.* The legal framework was put in place in 2003; an e-Id card is being introduced along with the e-passport.

xxi.   *Portugal.* The e-ID card has a chip and a magnetic strip for storing personal information and biometric data. The biometric data will initially be fingerprints but can be extended at a later date to include other biometrics such as iris scans.

xxii. *Sweden.* The e-passport introduced in October 2005 met the ICAO facial recognition standards and the USA visa waiver program requirements. A facial image is stored on a RFID microchip in the passport. Alongside the e-passport and e-ID card was also issued.

xxiii. *Slovakia.* Biometric passports implementation strategy has been put in place, to speed up the implementation process.

xxiv. *Slovenia.* The e-passports were issued from September 2006, which currently consist of a digital facial image a further biometric fingerprint will be added in March 2008.

xxv.   *United Kingdom.* There has been fierce debate over the introduction of E-Id cards; the UK currently is unique in Europe in not having an identity card. The ultimate decision on whether a biometric ID card will be implemented is still uncertain. Biometric passports have begun to be issued; the service is being rolled out across local enrolment centres across the UK during 2007. From 2008 the 7 million people who apply for a passport each year will also receive an e-id card.

In 2006, the British Parliament passed legislation to introduce biometric-based national identity (or ID) cards. The government has touted the cards as a means to reduce identity fraud, reduce illegal immigration to the United Kingdom, and help in the reduction of organized crime and terrorism, among other benefits. Under a timetable set out when the legislation was passed, from 2008 onwards, everyone renewing a passport will be issued an ID card and have his or her personal information (including biometric data) placed in an associated database – the National Identity Register. The biometric portion of the system will likely use face recognition, fingerprints and iris scans. Later on, the government plans to introduce stand-alone identity cards for people who do not want a passport. Until 2010, people can choose not to have an ID card, though they will still have to pay for one, and will still be placed in the database. Possessing an identity card will eventually become compulsory. Concerns related to the accuracy and vulnerability of biometric systems has been raised with respect to the national identity cards scheme. A report (LSE, 2005) released by researchers at the London School of Economics and Political Science (LSE) prior to the passage of the legislation suggested that the technology at the core of the scheme has been untested on the scale proposed by the United Kingdom's Home Office, and that the database with the details of every ID card holder is likely to become a major target for security attacks. Another report, by a House of Commons committee, noted that there was a lack of transparency surrounding the incorporation of scientific advice, and that "choices regarding biometric technology have preceded trials" (House of Commons Science and Technology Committee, 2006). Although there are privacy concerns related to the identity cards proposal, much of the criticism of the scheme has centred on its cost. For example, the LSE report estimated that the scheme's implementation and running costs would be in the range of £10.6 billion to £19.2 billion (approximately C$22.3 billion to $40.4 billion) over the first 10 years (at 2005-2006 prices) (LSE, 2005). This estimate is considerably higher than the government's estimate of £584 million a year (UK Home Office, 2005a). In response to the LSE report, the Home Office branded the LSE's cost estimates as being "vague" and based on "misguided assumptions," (UK Home Office, 2005b) and provided an excerpt from another review that suggested that the methodology for the government's cost estimates was robust (KPMG, 2005). The government later clarified that its figure applied only to the annual operating cost of the scheme for the lead department (the Home Office). Although the government has not provided a final estimate of the total cost of the scheme, because it deems that information to be commercially sensitive, the legislation requires the government to provide an estimate to Parliament every six months on the public expenditure likely to be incurred on the ID cards scheme. The UK Home Office suggest that the identity cards scheme, at least in its present form, may be in trouble. According to these reports, the timetable for introduction of the cards is under review as part of an examination of all Home Office operations (Ford, 2006). The British Ex-Prime Minister (Tony Blair) has stressed, however, that the biometric-based ID card will go ahead, and that it is a major plank of the Labour Party's manifesto for the next U.K. general election.

6.   IMPACTS OF FUTURE BIOMETRICS TECHNOLOGIES

The future biometrics technologies hope to bring accuracy with the least amount of personal intrusion as possible. The following biometric technologies are the new generation of identification and verification methods for the 21st centaury (Purdue University, 2001; Secguide, 2001; Shoniregun, 2005):

i. The *vein pattern identification* technology is like a retinal scan. It uses special light to produce an image of the vein pattern in the face, wrist, or hand. An advantage to this technology is that veins are stable throughout ones life and cannot be tampered with.

ii. The *ear shape identification* is unique as a fingerprint. This technology is for measuring the geometry of the ear.

iii. The *body odour identification* technology uses a sensor to identify the body odour and stores it in a digital database. The technology is under development and when released may be too expensive.

iv. The *body salinity identification* exploits the natural level of salinity in the human body, which is accomplished by an electric field that passes a tiny electrical current through the body. As of now, individual's salinity levels are believed to be unique, but biometric identification is not the only use that we may benefit from this emerging technology. The electrical current, which passes through the body, can also carry data. The transfer rate is equivalent to 2400-baud modem. This technology could include interaction between communication devices carried on the body such as watches and mobile phones.

The future of biometrics holds great promise for law enforcement applications, as well for private industry uses. The following scenarios presents some of the problematic nature of biometrics applications.

Scenario 1. Within the car industry a biometric verification system is under evaluation. Manufacturers of expensive cars are considering using fingerprint recognition as a requirement for ignition of the engine. On the other hand, suppose that the righteous owner of a car cannot use his car because his fingerprint is rejected. The car owner will consider this to be a much more serious flaw in the system than a technical failure which prevents the car from being started. This is especially true if he compares the advantages of this system with this rejection: the advantages are that the driver does not (necessarily) have to have a key to his car and a perception of higher security with respect to theft of his car. Whether the security improves is questionable. Right now, we do not see car thieves trying to copy the key of your car; instead they try to by-pass the ignition mechanism where the car key is involved. Furthermore, it might decrease security since it is fairly easy and cheap to copy a fingerprint from a person, even without the person knowing this.

Scenario 2. Suppose that a bank decides that for transactions, which exceed a certain amount of money, identification of the employee performing the transaction is required. The argumentation to use fingerprint verification instead of for example username/password combinations are that in the case of fingerprint verification, the employee has to be present and cannot transfer his username/password to a colleague to perform transactions for him. Other systems that are considered, such as smart cards, can also not prevent the employee from letting other people perform a transaction. The bank trusts on the solution presented to them and decides to rollout the fingerprint verification system throughout all offices. An employee of the bank knows that these systems can be circumvented and decides to make a dummy from a fingerprint of a colleague. The risks are small since using the fingerprint of a colleague cannot be traced back to him. To obtain the fingerprint he asks the colleague whose fingerprint he intends to use to hand him a glass or plate. This will almost certainly leave a perfect print on a clean surface, with which a dummy can be created and the fraudulent transactions can be performed. In case the malicious employee is not capable of creating a good dummy, he/she can always perform transactions using his own finger and claim that a colleague frames him/her.

However, as the need increases for government bodies and large firms to deploy hi-tech security systems to solve crimes or protect employees, biometric technology will improve, as investor confidence increases. Once the consumer confidence is evident, biometric research will provide further innovations, which will in turn strengthen future performance, and this cycle will continue to build in a positive direction. The ISO/IEC JTC1 is the governing body of international biometric standards. The standardisation is still in progress. We have foreseen that in the future, fixed biometric standards will be in place to guide vendors and developers in the areas of biometric application profiles, interfaces, and system performance. But the impact of biometrics technology on privacy varies, depending on how and where they are deployed. Biometrics in itself is not a privacy risk but the relationship between the type of biometric and the way in which it is deployed determines the relationship between biometrics and privacy. The 'BioPrivacy Application Impact Framework' is a tool, which can be used to determine the potential impact of a biometric application on privacy. The criteria assessed are as follows:

i   *Overt/Covert.* Overt deployments ensure the user is aware of the systems operation and that data is being collected and used with their consent. Covert deployments do not require consent from the user and should only be implemented in areas where there is a compelling reason to check a persons identity.

ii. *Optional/Mandatory.* A mandatory system where users are required to consent to be enrolled in the system such as company's employees' or a state id card or passport system. An optional system as the name suggests requires the user to give consent to their data being stored. Mandatory systems as would be expected are less trusted since the collection of the data is imposed on the user. For both types of system protection, measures must be put into operation and also there can be punitive actions, which can be taken by the organisation to encourage enrolment.

iii. *Verification/Identification.* The biometric systems, which require a 1:N search that is susceptible to privacy, related issues and require more strict protection measures than a system, which uses a 1:1 search.

iv. *Fixed Period/Indefinite Deployment.* The short-term deployment will offer fewer privacy risks. A long-term deployment such as a public surveillance system, in contrast is more likely to have a negative impact on privacy. A permanent deployment is also susceptible to function creep where more and more cases of identification are carried out and a number of related databases may be linked to give a body access to data which they previously did not have access to. Most systems in use are for an indefinite period. A balance needs to be reached between a reduction in personal privacy and an increase in the privacy of information.

v. *Private/Public Sectors.* Governments must collect biometric and other data under strict controls and restrictions. Private sector companies can link or share personal data for marketing and profiling purposes. Whatever the environments into which biometrics has be implemented adequate protection, a transparent procedures need to be implemented.

vi. *Individual Customer/Employee or Citizen.* The role of the user varies, so the right to privacy should be universal regardless of the organisation with which the user interacts. The expectation of the levels of privacy, which the user expects, depends on the organisation they are interacting with. It is also important that data held in separate biometric systems should not be shared, linked or amalgamated without the permission of the individual.

vii. *Enrolee/Institution.* A deployment, which allows the user to maintain ownership of the biometric information, is likely to offer greater privacy protection when compared to a public or private institution, which owns the data. It is equally arguable to say that individual biometrics profile does not belong to any organisations neither does it belongs to the government.

viii. *Personal Storage/Database Storage.* This refers to where the biometric data is held; information, which is stored centrally, is more likely to be abused compared to biometric data, which is held on a PC or a smart card. The privacy risks in biometrics are determined by the location of template storage and processing.

ix. *Behavioural/Physiological* biometric such as voice and signature scan are less likely to be deployed in a fashion which would invade privacy since voice and signature can easily be altered by changing the pass phrase or the style of the signature. Behavioural biometrics technologies are less likely to be used in 1:N applications because of the laxity.

x. *Templates/Identifiable Images*. Privacy risks are greater where the biometric images are stored in the database as opposed to the storage of a biometric template of the biometric. Biometric templates are only of value when the vendor algorithm is also supplied and is linked to a specific biometric. Biometrics held as images are generally identifiable and can be associated with a specific individual and a visual or aural inspection.

The BioPrivacy Impact Framework is a means of determining the privacy risks of a biometric deployment to the individual users (see Table 6-1 for further details). The minimum impact on privacy is achieved by a private sector application where the user retains ownership of their biometric. The largest effect on privacy would be from a covert surveillance system. The effects of other system would fall somewhere between the two extremes. Whatever the system, which is to be deployed precautions, must be taken to safeguard privacy, these precautions must be proportionate to the potential risks, which the system may encounter. Additional factors must also be taken into account such as the political climate, political system and the legal aspects, which apply to biometrics. This framework could be just as part of the initial analysis of the risks posed by implementing biometrics, but it should be used in conjunction with other forms of analysis. The views of the members of the public and the potential users should also be taken into account, since it is better to implement a system with the cooperation of the user than to impose a system which ids not trusted onto a hostile public.

Table 5–1. BioPrivacy application impact framework

Low	Risk of privacy invasion	High
Overt	Are the users aware of the systems operation?	Covert
Optional	Is the system optional or mandatory?	Mandatory
Verification	Is the system used for identification or verification	Identification
Fixed Period	What period of time is the deployment for?	Indefinite
Private Sector	Is the deployment public or private?	Public Sector
Individual, Customer	In what capacity is the user interacting with the system?	Employee, Citizen
Enrolee	Who owns the biometric information?	Institution
Personal Storage	Where is the biometric data held?	Database Storage
Behavioural	What type of biometric technology is being deployed?	Physiological
Templates	Does the system utilise biometric templates, biometric images or both?	Images

Under British law there is no definition of privacy and an individual has no automatic right to privacy. The two types of privacy that needs to be considered are individual and information privacy. Personal privacy assumes that a person should not be subjected to unwarranted intrusion, both physical such as directly being observed or at a distance such as unauthorised access to personal data held on someone. The privacy of information, which is held on an individual, assumes that data will be held in a secure manner and access will be limited to those who the individual has approved to be allowed access. All the requests to prove identity are treated with mistrust to different degrees. One of the most distrusted forms of identification is biometrics; this is due to it being a new technology and the fact that it can often appear intrusive. At the moment it is possible for people to adopt different identities for different situations, e.g. at work, at home or on the internet, but if a biometric identifier needs to be given this can only apply to one specific individual. As biometric devices become more affordable and their use increases it will be more difficult to remain anonymous.

The most common concern about the use of biometrics is in what context they will be used. If information is collected by governments or has to be turned over to law enforcement bodies it may become possible to track peoples' every move and produce dossiers on everyone. This is also possible at the moment by using credit cards, oyster cards and mobile phones. Adding biometric collection into the equation will make it easier to track individual's movement. Biometrics technologies may be able to preserve privacy, since there are many different proprietary brands, which are not compatible; it may not be practicable to link them all together into an all-encompassing network. When biometrics are combined with encryption the data held on public and private databases could be prevented from being merged and prevents intrusion from outside bodies.

The increased collection of data on individuals is resulting in a loss of autonomy and people feel as if they have lost control of their identity to businesses and governments. There is a need for extra information to be provided for the confirmation of their identity. The real problem occurs when the collected data is not held securely and criminals gain access to the data and can use it for identity theft. Privacy concerns in biometrics are mainly concerned with the unauthorised and unnecessary collection of information. The unauthorised collection occurs when biometric data is collected without the knowledge of the individual, but it is rare in consumer applications. For positive identification a biometric will not always be necessary or multiple biometrics could be collected when just one would be sufficient. As technology developed there has been a temptation on the part of the holder of the biometric information to manipulate and analyse stored data. When a person submits their biometric for a particular function they give permission for its use in that area. It is easy for this biometrics to be used or disclosed without authority being sought from the individual. Biometrics is a new technology and many countries have not legislated on how, where and when the information can be used and distributed. The collection of the biometric is not an inherent invasion of privacy, but if the information is misused or disclosed to a third party it can result in identity theft. Trust can be engendered in this new technology if companies and government bodies have to get an individuals permission before data can be shared with another body. In practice this would be costly and time consuming, which will either result in data not being shared or companies will do it anyway and hope they do not get caught. A number of minimum personal requirements will need to be put into place if the public is to have trust in the application and the use of biometrics:

- Participation should be voluntary in consumer applications.

- Biometric data should be collected overtly with the full consent of the individual. Covert collection of biometric and secret databases should not exist in consumer applications.

- Consumer applications should not store the actual biometric, they should only be able to store an encrypted template.

- If a company requires biometrics it does not need to collect other information that it currently uses to confirm identity.

In ideal situations the individual should be informed of the specific reason the biometric is being used, collected and disclosed. They should also be made aware of the risks and benefits of participation and non-participation. The individual's consent should be obtained and laws should be drafted and implemented to cover the challenges which biometrics are making on individual privacy.

7.   SUMMARY OF CHAPTER FIVE

In 2002, the Canadian Minister for Citizenship and Immigration, Denis Coderre, called for a public debate on the introduction of a national identity card containing biometric identifiers. The debate occurred, in part, via hearings conducted by the House of Commons Standing Committee on Citizenship and Immigration. The Committee's interim report, tabled in 2003, detailed several concerns about a national identity card system and concluded that a much broader public debate was necessary to decide on the merits of a national identity card itself. If the card were deemed necessary, the Committee noted that other issues such as the financial cost of an identity card system, the nature of the biometric technology to be employed, the security of personal data, and other privacy issues also had to be addressed. The Committee did not table a final report on the national identity card scheme. Following the June 2004 general election, the issue disappeared from the federal government's agenda. The way biometric documents have been implemented in each European country is highly variable and has been influenced by the culture of each state. For implementation to be successful and uniform, governments still have a lot of work to do to convince the people of the advantages of such technologies. The international collaboration will eventually lead to the development of standards that will ease the deployment of biometrics. Some countries such as the Nordic area have cooperated to produce a single standard for their biometric documents, but it would be better if Europe wide standard can be integrated. A Europe-wide standard will reduce costs and also allow for cross border legislation to be put into place to safeguard privacy and govern how the technology can be used (House of Commons Standing Committee on Citizenship and Immigration, 2003). But if biometrics is the way forward the questions to ask are: *'How much will it cost to implement biometrics security solutions?'*, *'Who should be trusted with genetics information?'* and *'How long will it take the expert hacker to decrypt human genetic codes?'*.

Finally, the next chapter concludes the study carried out in this book.

REFERENCES

Acharya, L., 2006, *Biometrics and Government*, http://www.parl.gc.ca/informatio n/library/PRBpubs/prb0630-e.pdf, (April 3, 2007).

Argenbright, G., 2006, *Saflink SureAccess Reader Can Improve Security at Seaports, Airports and Other Critical Facilities*, http://www.saflink.com/ (November 15, 2006).

B&J Biometrics, Inc., 2006, *Releases New Ultra Biometric Fingerprnt Encryption Mouse*, http://www.biometrics-bj.com; http://news.thomasnet.com/fullstory/501662; and http://fingerprint.nist.gov/minex04 (February 20, 2007).

Bradt, G., 2006, *Silex technology launches first biometric WiFi access control device*, Press Release: http://www.silexamerica.com/us/about/news/press.html (February 27, 2007).

CEIS (Commissioner for enterprise and information society), 2004, *Conference on Biometrics for the benefit of the citizen: a European Perspective*, Contribution By Ján Figel', Phoenix Park, Dublin.

Clement, A., and Boa, K., 2006, *Developing Canada's Biometric Passport: Where are Citizens in this Picture?*,

Conforti, M., 2007, *Fidelica Microsystems Announces Release of Fingerprint Authentication Platform*, Press Release: http://www.fidelica.com/ (March 7, 2007).

Council Regulation (EC) 2004, *Standards for Security Features and Biometrics in Passports and Travel Documents Issued by Member States*, No 2252/2004 of 13 December.

DeFina, F, 2006, *New Panasonic Iris Reader Delivers Faster, More Accurate Access Control Identification and Authentication*, http://www.panasonic.com/sec urity (September 27, 2006).

Ford, R., 2006, *ID cards under threat in review of Home Office*, Times Online, 12 July 2006.

Grijpink, J., 2001, *Biometrics and Privacy*, Computer Law and Security Report, Volume 17, Issue 3, May.

House of Commons Science and Technology Committee, 2006, *Identity Card Technologies: Scientific Advice, Risk and Evidence* (PDF), Sixth Report of Session 2005-2006, August 2006.

House of Commons Standing Committee on Citizenship and Immigration, 2003, *A National Identity Card for Canada?*, http://www.oipcbc.org/pdfs/public/cimmrp06-e.pdf, (March 4, 2007).

International Biometric Group, 2005, *BioPrivacy Application Impact Framework*, http://www. biometricgroup.com (May 07, 2007)

KPMG, 2005, *Home Office ID Cards Programme Cost Methodology and Cost Review Outline Business Case Review* (PDF), Published Extract, November.

LSE, 2005, Identity Project 2005, *The Identity Project: an assessment of the UK Identity Cards Bill and its implications* (PDF), London School of Economics and Political Science, June.

Lundquist, E., 2007, *Kwikset(R) Introduces Futuristic New Biometric Home Security Application*, http://www.Kwikset.com, (March 18, 2007).

Morrison, R., 2006, *id-Confirm(TM) Unveils Portable, Turnkey Biometric Solution to Financial Fraud and Identity Theft*, http://www.id-confirm.com/index.php (December 30, 2006).

Najm, C., 2006, *Cryptolex Trust Systems Unveils New Approach to Secure Identity Verification*, http://www.cryptolex.com (November 2, 2006).

Office of the Privacy Commissioner of Canada, 2006, *Information from media lines*, July.

Pertsov, P., 2007, *Biometric Offering for AD Opens the New BioLink IDenium Product Line*, Press Release: http://www.biolinksolutions.com (March 28, 2007).

Prabhakar, S., Pankanti, S., and Jain, A., 2003, 'Biometric Recognition: Security and Privacy Concerns', *IEEE security and Privacy*, march/April.

Purdue University, 2001, *Match Future Biometric Technologies*, http://tech.purdue.edu (March 11, 2007).

Richard, D., 2006, *Atmel's New FingerChip Sensor Targets Physical Access Control Devices*, http://www.atmel.com/dyn/products/datasheets.asp?family_id= 609 (March 19, 2007).

Roberts, B., 2003, 'Are you ready for biometrics', *HR Magazine*, Mar 2003, Volume 48, Issue 3.

Royal Canadian Mounted Police (RCMP), 2006, *THE RTID REPORT*, http://www.rcmp-grc. gc.ca /rtid/report_issue1_e.htm (April 1, 2007).

Ruggles, T., 2006, CSC *Announces New Identity Management and Credentialing Solution*, http://www.csc.com (September 20, 2006).

Secguide, 2001, *Biometric Technologies*, http://www.secguide.com/editorIal_a rticles/biometric_technologies.htm (March 17, 2007).

Shoniregun, C. A., 2005, *Impacts and Risk Assessment of Technology for Internet Security: Enable information Small-medium Enterprises (TEISMEs)*, Springer, New York, USA.

Sparapani, T.D., 2006, *On Secure Flight and Registered Traveler Before the U.S. Senate Committee on Commerce, Science and Transportation*, ACLU Legislative Counsel, February.

Statewatch News editorial, 2006, *EU-Passports*, July, www.statewatch.org/news/2006/ jul/04eubio-passport.htm (March 20, 2007).

Stryczek, M., 2006, *American Barcode and RFID Announces TETRAGATE, which Links Biometric Facial Recognition and RFID, Creating Formidable Security Solution*, Press Release: http://www.amerbar.com/ (February 2, 2007).

UK Home Office, 2005a, *Regulatory Impact Assessment* (PDF), May.

UK Home Office, 2005b, *Home Office Response to The London School of Economics' ID Cards Cost Estimates & Alternative Blueprint* (PDF), July.

United States Department of Homeland Security, 2005, *Transportation Security Administration, Statement of Kip Hawley, Assistant Secretary before the Subcommittee on Economic Security, Infrastructure Protection and Cybersecurity, Committee on Homeland Security, United States House of Representatives*, November.

United States Government Accountability Office, 2006, *Homeland Security: Recommendations to Improve Management of Key Border Security Program Need to Be Implemented*, February.

Chapter 6

CONCLUSION

The chapter 1 has set the background for this research, while chapters 2 and 3 discuss the biometrics measurements and the risk applications. The two latter chapters have given the foundation of the study, which are further explored by using the research methods suggested to capture the experiences and the views of businesses, governments and society. The chapter 4 focuses on the techniques of acquiring data and information for the procurement of knowledge. The methods and methodologies adopted aids in studying the subject matter. Both quantitative and qualitative processes of collecting data were employed which encourages a rich mixture of analysis and conclusive findings. The chapter 4 further presents SCSBAM and chapter 5 critically evaluates the research area. However, this chapter concludes with recommendation, contribution to knowledge and future work.

1. OPERATIONAL ISSUES OF BIOMETRICS

The word biometrics is very often used as a synonym for the perfect security. This is a misleading view. There are numerous conditions that must be taken in account when designing a secure biometric system. Firstly, it is necessary to realise that biometrics are not secrets. This implies that biometric measurements cannot be used as capability tokens, they are not secure for generating cryptographic keys either. Secondly, it is necessary to trust the input device and make the communication link secure. And thirdly, the input device needs to check the livelyness of the person being measured and the device itself should be verified by a challenge-response protocol.

The question of maximum limits on user enrolment can be critical to large-scale systems. Limitations differ for verification and identification systems. Certain types of verification systems have no limits on potential growth. In a 1:1 system wherein matching takes place on a local PC or biometric reader, there is effectively no restriction on the number of users a system might incorporate. However, problems do occur with different positioning on the acquiring sensor, imperfect imaging conditions, environmental changes, deformations, noise and bad user interaction with the sensor, it is impossible that two samples of the same biometric characteristic, acquired in different sessions, exactly coincide. For this reasons, a biometric matching system's response is typically matched with a score (normally a single number) that quantifies the similarity between the input and the database template representations. The similarity score s is compared with an acceptance threshold t and if s is greater than or equal to t then the compared samples belong to the same person. Pairs of biometric samples generating scores lower than t belong to a different person. The distribution of scores generated from pairs of samples from different persons is called an *impostor distribution*, and the score distribution generated from pairs of samples of the same person is called a *genuine distribution* (Prabhakar et al., 2003; Delac and Grgic, 2004). The main system errors are usually measured in terms of:

- FNMR (*false non-match rate*): mistaking two biometrics measurements from the same person to be from two different persons.

- FMR (*false match rate*): mistaking biometric measurement from two different people to be the same.

FNMR and FMR are basically functions of the system threshold t: if the system's designers decrease t to make the system more tolerant to input variations and noise, FMR increases. On the other hand, if they raise t to make the system more secure, FNMR increases accordingly. FMR and FNMR are brought together in a receiver operating characteristic (ROC) curve that plots the FMR against FNMR (or 1-FNMR) at different thresholds (Prabhakar et al., 2003).

Indeed, much attention has been paid to biometrics as a way forward in securing the society against terror as a means of increasing security in public places and for businesses transactions. Biometrics technology is superior to other identification solutions because it verifies a person's identity based on a unique physical attribute rather than some paper or plastic ID card, and as such, the number of biometric implementations is on the rise. Public awareness and acceptance of biometrics is increasing steadily as well. With as little as a home address, driver's license number or bank account number, criminals can use the Internet to find out all kinds of personal information about an individual. In some US prisons, visitors to inmates are subject to verification procedures in order that identities are not swapped during the visit. Criminals can obtain the necessary data to get new credit cards issued in your name, print fake cheques in your name, obtain bank loans in your name, and perpetrate other creative identity theft scams in your name to profit at your expense. By the time one finds out what has happened, serious damage can be done. Victims of identity theft often spend years and thousands of dollars clearing their names and credit reports.

The implementation of payment-processing systems that utilise biometrics with private account management can easily prevent online credit card fraud. Biometrics can be incorporated at the point of sale, thereby enabling consumers to enrol their payment options e.g., checking, credit, debit, loyalty, etc., into a secure electronic account that is protected by, and accessed with, a unique physical attribute such as a fingerprint. Cash, cards or cheque are not needed to make purchases, so there is no need to carry them in a purse or wallet. Not carrying a purse or wallet eliminates the chances of it being stolen or lost while shopping. The biometrics transaction-processing systems well suited for personal cheque use. Biometrics can also offer increased protection for check-cashing services, whether personal or payroll. By requiring biometric identity verification before allowing a check to be cashed, the possibility of it being presented by anyone other than the intended payee is eliminated. A biometrics verification and identification can ensure that a person is who he or she claims to be, or can identify a person from a database of trusted or suspect individuals. If the identity of a traveller or employee is in question, biometrics can be a highly effective solution. An individual using a forged or stolen badge or ID card, if required to verify biometrically before entering a secure area, would likely be detected if his/her biometric does not match the biometric on file. An individual claiming a fraudulent ID can be identified from a database of known criminals and linked to biometric identification systems, which may prevent him or her from boarding an airplane. The barrier in growth of biometrics is the costs of implementation and connectivity speed of services, and reliable authentication. For fingerprint scanning, as people become older and loose the fat in their skin, the fingerprints become worn out, this makes it difficult for the scanner to read the image. Research has proved that some biometrics features are expensive and less accurate in result such as hand scan. There could be some false rejection because of external environment factors. For example, lightening may affects the result of face scanning. External noise can affect the authentication of voice recognition. However, voice changes with the passage of time due to different factors (flu, soar throat or emotional conditions) can affect the voice recognition pattern.

2. RECOMMENDATION

The Internet is a worldwide network of insecurely connected networks that are extremely easy to gain access through a host computer. The unauthorized access to information is very easy and is very hard to catch the intruders. The computer connected to the Internet can be a weak link, allowing unauthorized access to both individuals and organisations information irrespective of location. This research recommends that the Internet security vendors, organisations, and governments should target the following areas:

i.   Aligning biometrics applications security with generic security approach.

ii. Exploiting biometric applications security issues and available tools for competitive advantage.

iii. Create efficient and effective way of managing biometrics security issues.

iv. Continuous improvement of security policies that will be dynamically enhance existing biometric applications (see Chapters 4 and 5 for further discussion).

It has been suggested by Shoniregun (2007) that the first two areas above concerned with information security strategy, the third with managing Internet security, and fourth with adopted security policies.

3. CONTRIBUTION TO KNOWLEDGE

The extensive literature research revealed that biometrics should be combined with other security technologies in order to achieve fairly secured operations. The contributions of this research to knowledge are:

i.   Conceptual ideology of biometrics.

ii. Classification and taxonomy of biometrics.

iii. Impacts of biometrics on society.

iv. Lack existing model on how best to secure biometrics applications.

v. Synchronising biometrics with generic security approach.

This study will help in addressing the critical issues facing biometrics' users, and security professionals as they endeavour to implement biometrics. It also provides a window on the future understanding of the limitation of biometrics. Moreover, the SCSBAM has been designed to provide a one-stop shop reference on how biometrics applications can be made secured. Thus the studies of the biometrics are not simple, but are necessary for the users, ISPs, organisations, and the governments in understanding the security limitations of biometrics performance —however, there are still many challenges confronting biometrics!

4. Future work

It is noted that many other factors are relevant to the successful implementation of biometrics. The immediate future work will investigate the fault tolerance of biometrics platform integration.

REFERENCES

Delac, K., and Grgic, M., 2004, *A survey of biometric recognition methods*, 46th International Symposium Electronics in Marine, ELMAR-2004, June, Zadar, Croatia

Prabhakar, S., Pankanti, S., Jain, A.K., 2003, *Biometric Recognition: Security and Privacy Concerns*, IEEE Security & Privacy, March/April.

Shoniregun, C.A., 2007, *Lecture: Impacts of Biometrics on the Society*, University of East London (UeL), London, UK.

INDEX